JUNE KIMMEL

My Heart
RESTORED

JOURNEYFORTH
Greenville, South Carolina

Library of Congress Cataloging-in-Publication Data

Kimmel, June, 1955-
  My heart restored / June Kimmel.
      p. cm.
  Summary: "My Heart Restored is a book for women who are weary
and need encouragement and healing through the restorative steps of
Bible study and prayer"—Provided by publisher.
  ISBN 978-1-59166-925-8 (perfect bound pbk. : alk. paper)
1. Christian women—Religious life. 2. Spiritual healing—Biblical
teaching. 3. Encouragement—Biblical teaching. I. Title.
  BV4527.K4747 2008
  248.8'43—dc22

                                                             2008030479

My Heart Restored

Design by Rita Golden
Page layout by Kelley Moore

© 2009 by BJU Press
Greenville, South Carolina 29614
JourneyForth Books is a division of BJU Press

Printed in the United States of America
All rights reserved

ISBN 978-1-59166-925-8

15   14   13   12   11   10   9   8   7   6   5   4   3   2   1

The Lord is my Shepherd;
I shall not want.
He maketh me to lie down in green pastures:
He leadeth me beside the still waters.
He restoreth my soul.

Contents

My Rocking Chair

My rocking chair became my oasis—the escape that my weary heart desperately needed. There was nothing magical or unique about my rocker; but its leather covering and wooden frame became my refuge, my hiding place. In this chair, God met me as I opened the pages of His Word to discover the comfort and encouragement that my overwrought soul required. From this chair, I spared my heavenly Father no detail of the agony and struggle I felt within my frantic heart. Nothing happening around me mattered. Once seated, my focus was heavenward. During the countless, silent hours in that chair, I caught a new glimpse of my Savior.

My children refer to those months as "the summer Mom cried." My husband and I had been in full-time ministry for almost twenty years. After five years at this church, I found myself spiritually, emotionally, and physically exhausted. Why? I was trying to be everything—pastor's wife, mother of three, Christian schoolteacher, church organist, Sunday school teacher, Bible study teacher, women's counselor. I was getting up by 5:30 every morning to be sure I had my time with the Lord. My grueling schedule had rendered me fragile, weary, and lonely.

When summer finally arrived that year, my father-in-law carried my rocking chair to my bedroom for me and I began my recovery. Each morning after the children had started their activities for the day, I would spend the next couple of hours in my rocker reading God's Word and praying. Utterly consumed with the need to sit at Jesus' feet, I allowed Him to minister to my weary soul. He began to quiet my anxious heart and surround me with His strong and loving arms. He impressed upon me the need to stop doing things for Him and start loving and worshiping Him. My busyness was good, but I was missing God's best—Himself!

Every morning of that long, difficult summer, God met me as I went to my quiet refuge. He ministered to my weary heart and taught me about Himself through His precious Word. After I had read my Bible and prayed, I would read books that focused on God—*The Knowledge of the Holy, Knowing God, A Woman After God's Own Heart*. The more I meditated on my Lord, the stronger I became.

In that rocking chair over ten years ago, God began the study *That I May Know Him*. I didn't realize it then, but He wanted me to focus on Him alone so that I could challenge women all across the world to know Him better. The Lord showed me Who He is and Who He desires to be in my life. Philippians 3:10 became my prayer: "That I may know him, and the power of his resurrection, and the fellowship of his sufferings, being made conformable unto his death."

When I ended that summer, my weary soul was refreshed. With my focus renewed, I saw Him not only as my Savior but also as my

Refuge, my Friend, my Comfort, my Strength, and much more. The Lord had shown me through His Word the meaning of Psalm 23:3—"He restoreth my soul"—that only a loving and gracious God could take my exhausted soul and restore it. I still had some physical issues that had to be addressed, but my fellowship with the Savior was renewed. Job 42:5 explains what happened to me that summer: "I have heard of thee by the hearing of the ear, but now mine eye seeth thee." The weariness of my heart had slowed down my life for me to better see my Lord. Since that summer, I daily revisit these truths. This restoration is a continual process as I seek to walk in daily communion with the Lord.

I've realized that my weariness of soul is not rare. Christian women need refreshing encouragement! It is easy to be over-whelmed with the cares and demands of life. No matter our age or responsibilities, we all can be "weary in well doing" (2 Thessalonians 3:13). These times of discouragement should not surprise us. But when we do struggle, how we deal with them will determine their impact on our lives. How do you respond? How do your thoughts and your actions change? How long does it take for you to again rest confidently in the Lord?

Through the pages of this book, you will be challenged to confront your weary heart and to see God's solutions. Since God alone is our sufficiency and source of true restoration, we will consider what He graciously provides for us to have victory over discouragement and frustration. Chapter 2 will help you recognize the characteristics of a heart that needs this healing touch from the Lord. Several Bible characters illustrate our common struggles. Through the trying times they faced, we'll learn how God refreshed them with His gentle love and grace.

Once we identify our weary hearts, we will consider what God has provided to give us healing and encouragement. The trials we face are actually gracious acts used by the Master for our spiritual growth. Only when we stand in His presence will we be completely free from conflict and fully comprehend His victory. Until that glorious day, let's learn to use what He graciously provides to restore our weary hearts.

Do I Need Restoring?

CHAPTER TWO

In a moment's notice, the course of our lives can be dramatically altered. A loved one is taken in an accident, financial stability is relinquished with a phone call, and apparent good health is replaced by one diagnosis. Trials often leave us discouraged and exhausted.

It may be the conflicts around the world that trouble you. Countries war against each other while religious sects and political parties within a nation struggle for power. The battles may be closer to home with families striving to keep communication and relationships intact.

As individuals, our circumstances can quickly devour us—draining every ounce of resolve and strength. The stress of daily life devastates while the mundane seems pointless. Life feels empty and burdens nearly suffocate. We endeavor to keep going, but a weariness of heart leaves us exhausted physically, mentally, and spiritually.

With our joy and strength shattered, where can we turn? What is it that we need?

Our Lord is the One we should turn to when our attitudes and perspectives need to change. When we admit we are weak, He can restore our weary heart and give us purpose and strength. Restoring the soul is the "rekindling or quickening of the exhausted spirit."[1] The first step to restoration is to recognize that our fatigued spirits need the Lord's restorative touch.

> **The Lord Jesus is the source and power of**
> **true restoration for our weary hearts.**

Let's look at several people from the Bible who had struggles. Their details may be different from ours, but their hopelessness reflects what we often experience. As you consider these people, ask the Lord to reveal your needs and His solutions.

●⟩⟩⟩⟩ ●⟩⟩⟩⟩ HE RESTORES ME WHEN I FEEL ALONE ⟨⟨⟨⟨● ⟨⟨⟨⟨●

TIME OF GREAT VICTORY

Elijah, a prophet of God, had a deep impact on the nation of Israel. Under the rule of wicked King Ahab and Queen Jezebel, God's people suffered greatly; but Elijah stood fearlessly against their idolatrous practices. In 1 Kings 18, Elijah defied the prophets of Baal by challenging them to prove their god's power. After Elijah's sacrifice and altar were consumed by fire from heaven, he sealed this great victory by killing the false religious leaders and praying for God to send rain to end the drought and famine.

TIME OF WEARINESS

One would think after such a great victory that Elijah would revel in the conquest. But the opposite was true. Jezebel sent word to Elijah that he would soon be slain in the same way he had killed her prophets. In fear, Elijah ran into the wilderness. After a day's travel, Elijah fell exhausted under the shady branches of a juniper tree. He announced to God, "It is enough; now, O Lord, take away my life; for I am not better than my fathers" (1 Kings 19:4). With his strength gone, Elijah collapsed into a deep sleep. Three times an angel awakened him to nourish him with heavenly food. This food and rest sustained Elijah for forty days and nights as he made his way to Mount Sinai. While spending the night in a cave at this historic mount, God asked Elijah why he was there. He proudly declared with a well-rehearsed complaint that he alone was faithfully serving God. He wanted to die rather than continue this lonely battle.

TIME OF ENCOURAGEMENT

God then sent Elijah to the top of the mountain for an unforgettable exercise. Elijah needed to see God. Elijah had let the idol worshipers eclipse his view of the greatness of God. God used the power of nature to sharpen Elijah's senses. A strong wind tore the rocks of the mountain, yet God was not in the wind. An earthquake was followed by fire, but God was not in either of these astonishing displays. It was the "still small voice" that revealed God's presence. God encouraged Elijah with the fact that seven thousand in Israel had not bowed to the idol, Baal. Although Elijah felt alone, he was part of a large group of faithful believers. God further encouraged Elijah by calling Elisha to minister with him.

We often think God's power is revealed only in the dramatic events of our lives—not in the times of silence. We, too, can become discouraged when we face trials seemingly alone. But we must remember that as God was faithful to Elijah so He is to us. We may seem to stand alone in the midst of the masses, but God is always with us. His quiet voice reassures our lonely heart if we will "be still, and know that [He is] God" (Psalm 46:10).

**When I feel alone (even in the midst
of a crowd), I need restored!**

❋≫≫ ❋≫≫ He Restores Me When I Fear People ≪≪❋ ≪≪❋

David Attacked by Others

Throughout his life, David faced dangerous circumstances. David's greatest adversaries were his family and friends—not the Philistines or other enemies of God. King Saul, who saw David as a threat to the throne, relentlessly pursued him. In 1 Samuel 21, David fled to Nob to find safety from the king in the home of Ahimelech the priest. While David was there, Doeg, Saul's servant, saw him and immediately told the king where David was. King Saul sent for Ahimelech and all his family. When Saul realized that David had received help from the priest, he gave the order for Ahimelech and his family to be killed. One of Ahimelech's sons, Abiathar, escaped to warn David. David's heart grieved for the loss of this family; the responsibility of their deaths weighed heavy on his heart.

During his own reign as king, David again had to flee Jerusalem. Absalom rebelled against David's rule and undermined his father's authority. Absalom stole the hearts of the people through cunning promises. When he had a sufficient following, Absalom went to Hebron and declared himself the new king. Rather than crushing this insurgence and endangering the people of Israel, David fled Jerusalem, voluntarily ending his rule. Absalom planned to pursue his father while he was unprotected, weak, and vulnerable. God used a loyal friend of King David to change Absalom's plan. The altered strategy led to David's safe return to the throne.

DAVID RESTORED BY GOD

David wrote Psalm 3 and Psalm 52 as a result of these events. These two psalms clearly portray the contrasts between David's enemies and his God.

David laments in Psalm 3, "Lord, how are they increased that trouble me! many are they that rise up against me. Many there be which say of my soul, There is no help for him in God." But, he continues, "O Lord, [Thou] art a shield for me; my glory, and the lifter up of mine head. I cried unto the Lord with my voice, and he heard me. . . . I laid me down and slept; I awaked; for the Lord sustained me. I will not be afraid of ten thousands of people, that have set themselves against me round about." Then David implores the Lord for deliverance: "Arise, O Lord; save me, O my God: for thou hast smitten all mine enemies upon the cheek bone; thou hast broken the teeth of the ungodly. Salvation belongeth unto the Lord: thy blessing is upon thy people."

In Psalm 52 David asks Doeg, Saul's servant, why he was proud of his actions. David points out, "Thy tongue deviseth mischiefs; like a sharp razor, working deceitfully. Thou lovest evil more than good; and lying rather than to speak righteousness. Thou lovest all devouring words, O thou deceitful tongue." Then David turns to God's judgment of Doeg's wickedness. "God shall likewise destroy thee for ever, he shall take thee away, and pluck thee out of thy dwelling place, and root thee out of the land of the living. The righteous also shall see, and fear, and shall laugh at him: lo, this is the man that made not God his strength; but trusted in the abundance of his riches, and strengthened himself in his wickedness." God, in His mercy, would allow David to see the triumph of righteousness and to offer a song of praise. "I am like a green olive tree in the house of God: I trust in the mercy of God for ever and ever. I will praise thee for ever, because thou hast done it: and I will wait on thy name; for it is good before thy saints."

People's words and actions can easily turn our hearts from trusting God. Their opinions become more important to us than the desires of God. We fear man instead of fearing God. We feel insignificant and vulnerable—our strength is too weak to stand against the attacks and demands of our enemy. God can restore our wavering spirit when we fear others.

**When I am afraid of the people around me
and what they are doing, I need restored!**

●〉〉〉 ●〉〉〉 HE RESTORES ME WHEN I FACE MY SIN 〈〈〈● 〈〈〈●
DAVID'S SIN

Instead of going out to war, David remained in Jerusalem. David sent Joab, his servants, and all the forces of Israel to fight the children of Ammon. David's sin began with lust when he saw Bathsheba from his rooftop. His heart went quickly from temptation to adultery and then to murder as he tried to cover his sins. David's sin ultimately led to the deaths of Uriah, Bathsheba's husband, and Bathsheba and David's baby.

In the New Testament, James outlines for us the progression of sin: "But every man is tempted, when he is drawn away of his own lust, and enticed. Then when lust hath conceived, it bringeth forth sin: and sin, when it is finished, bringeth forth death" (1:14–15). The steps from James are the ones that King David followed.

Step 1. Temptation Attracts—"every man is tempted"

2 Samuel 11:2—"David arose from off his bed, and walked upon the roof of the king's house: and from the roof he saw a woman washing herself."

Step 2. Lust Charms—"drawn away of his own lust, and enticed"

2 Samuel 11:2—"The woman was very beautiful to look upon."

Step 3. Lust Conceives—"when lust hath conceived"

    2 Samuel 11:3—"And David sent and inquired after the woman. And one said, Is not this Bathsheba . . . the wife of Uriah the Hittite? And David sent messengers, and took her."

Step 4. Sin Follows—"it bringeth forth sin"

    2 Samuel 11:4–5—"And she came in unto him, and he lay with her . . . And [she] conceived, and sent and told David, and said, I am with child."

Step 5. Death Results—"when it is finished, bringeth forth death"

    2 Samuel 11:16–17—"And it came to pass, when Joab observed the city, that he assigned Uriah unto a place where he knew that valiant men were. And the men of the city went out, and fought with Joab: and there fell some of the people of the servants of David; and Uriah the Hittite died also."

    2 Samuel 12:19—"When David saw that his servants whispered, David perceived that the child was dead: therefore David said unto his servants, Is the child dead? And they said, He is dead."

When God sent Nathan, the prophet, to King David to confront him about his sin, David did not deny his actions. When Nathan said, "You are the man" (2 Samuel 12:7), David confessed, "I have sinned against the Lord" (2 Samuel 12:13). David's response was sorrowful and his repentance was indisputable. He immediately and humbly sought God for forgiveness.

DAVID'S CONFESSION

David went to the Lord with a prayer of repentance and with a desire for cleansing. He poured out his grieving heart to God. If we carefully consider the verses of Psalm 51, we see the steps David took to know God's restoring. David shows us that those who have failed and fallen can be restored. "Have mercy upon me, O God, according to thy lovingkindness: according unto the multitude of thy tender mercies blot out my transgressions. Wash me throughly from mine iniquity, and cleanse me from my sin" (verses 1–2).

David used four terms of forgiveness in the first two verses of this psalm. His words left no room for misunderstanding as he opened his heart to God. He pleaded with God to have mercy on him, to blot out his sin, to wash away his iniquity, and to cleanse his sin. David came before God acknowledging his guilt and declaring his sin before a righteous and holy God. He then asked God to forgive him and renew his heart and spirit. David not only wanted God's forgiveness but he also wanted the joy of his salvation restored. David desired an inner revival of his wicked heart. He knew that God would forgive, restore, and uphold him. God would not reject the "broken spirit: a broken and a contrite heart" he was offering (Psalm 51:17). David then promised God his devoted service and continual praise.

When David faced his sin and confessed it, he was restored to sweet fellowship with God. Because of David's humble and repentant heart, he was described as being a man after God's own heart (Acts 13:22). Do you face your sin with candor, as David did? Frequently we hide behind the excuses we creatively invent to cover our sinful heart. With an air of spirituality, we enjoy identifying the iniquities of others but go to great effort to excuse our equally sinful actions. The guilt of sin weighs heavy under the convicting power of the Holy Spirit. We, like David, can know the joy of sins forgiven.

When I sin and my fellowship with
God is broken, I need restored!

❋ ❯❯❯ He Restores Me When I Am Fatigued in Battle ❮❮❮ ❋

Moses' Need

When Moses and the children of Israel wandered in the wilderness, they faced many incredible trials that required them to trust God. In the first seven verses of Exodus 17, God supplied the drinking water they desperately needed. God's provision came from a rock that He directed Moses to strike with his rod.

Soon after this miraculous display, Amalek, a nomadic tribe from this region, attacked Israel. This attack was both unprovoked and unprecedented. Moses told Joshua to choose men from among the people and lead them in the fight against Amalek. These men were not trained soldiers but obediently followed Joshua into battle. Moses, Aaron, and Hur went up to the top of a hill to observe the encounter.

When Moses held up his hands, Israel would overcome the soldiers of Amalek, but when Moses' arms became heavy and he relaxed, Amalek would take the advantage. When Moses could no longer extend his arms, Aaron and Hur devised a plan. They placed a stone under Moses for him to sit on, and they stood one on each side of him and held up his hands. Because Joshua and his men were victorious, Moses built an altar and named it Jehovah-Nissi, which means "the Lord my banner."[2]

Moses' Strength

Moses determined to remain obedient to God, but he found it physically impossible. Victory resulted because Aaron and Hur stood beside Moses and supported his weary arms. God used the encouragement of others to restore Moses. God used these faithful friends to give Moses the victory over physical fatigue and Joshua the victory over Israel's enemy.

When we face our daily battles, we need God's divine strength. When life brings weariness, God provides His gracious strength. Sometimes He sends us aid through dear Christian friends who encourage us as we minister to others. But ultimately, God is our Jehovah-Nissi, "our banner of victory," as He was for Moses![3]

When I am tired (of pain, sorrow, illness, disappointments, ineffectiveness, financial struggles, etc.), I need restored!

❀❯❯❯❯ ❀❯❯ HE RESTORES ME WHEN I AM FRUSTRATED ❮❮❀ ❮❮❮❮❀

MARTHA'S STRESS

We can easily identify with Martha. Most days include at least a few moments of stress. Our lives are surrounded with the latest conveniences promoted to make our lives easier and more efficient. But with each invention comes more to maintain. What is promoted to give us more time may actually rob us of the quiet moments we desperately need to keep a balance in our lives.

Martha's struggle came from wanting to serve a meal worthy of her guest. Her heart was flooded with anger and guilt because of the many details demanding her attention. She needed her sister's help! Was that too much to expect? How she must have resented the choice Mary had made. Martha, no doubt, desired to sit at Jesus' feet like her sister, but her guilt was hidden behind her misplaced priority.

Once when I was teaching this account to a group of women, I tried to summarize Martha's problem by using a menu analogy. I suggested that Martha should have prepared a casserole instead of meat and potatoes with all the trimmings. The alternate menu would have allowed her the opportunity to enjoy her honored guest. Although I realized that casseroles were invented centuries later, I felt rather clever for such a practical illustration. My creativeness was crushed when after the lesson one of the wives informed me that her husband didn't like casseroles. At least for her, the point of my modern parable was lost. The menu was not the real issue. Martha's choices were.

MARTHA'S PRIORITY

Martha lost the joy of serving and became frustrated with the demands she felt she carried. Martha needed restoring. When she voiced her annoyance with her sister, she also revealed her anger with Jesus. He seemingly had not recognized her need because He had not sent Mary to help. Jesus' loving rebuke may have startled Martha. His words revealed Martha's sin and challenged her wrong priorities and overwhelmed soul. Jesus identified the solution to Martha's problem. She needed to choose the one thing that was most important—learning of Him.

Martha had another opportunity to serve. In John 12:1–2, she again ministered to Jesus, but her attitude did not hinder her service. When we compare these two accounts, we see that Martha served again but with no apparent problem or frustration. She simply and graciously served—an evident sign that she had grown in her understanding of godly priorities. The meal must again be prepared, but this time it was not an opportunity for frustration but for loving service.

Do you take time to daily sit at Jesus' feet in Bible study, prayer, and meditation? What should you change in your life to put your priorities in Christ-honoring order? Would your ministry and other responsibilities be less overwhelming if you prefaced them with time at Jesus feet?

**When I become overwhelmed with all
I have to do, I need restored.**

My Heart Restored

God is

ready and

willing

to forgive

your sin

Spend time in prayer asking God to show you the reasons for your weariness. Take a few minutes to honestly evaluate your heart in light of God's servants that we have considered. God is ready and willing to forgive your sin, restore your fellowship, and renew your weary heart.

> Create in me a clean heart, O God; and renew a right spirit within me. Restore unto me the joy of thy salvation; and uphold me with thy free spirit. (Psalm 51:10, 12)

How parenthood has changed! With the birth of my two grand-daughters, I reentered the world of babies. How amazed I was at the vast assortment of baby necessities that had been invented since my youngest was born over two decades ago. The options and styles for any one thing are phenomenal. If an item survived this evolution, its features have been altered until it is almost beyond my recognition. And everything makes a noise or sings a song.

The advanced medical knowledge of prenatal development is also astounding. Probably the most significant change in the parenting prelude is the ability to identify the gender of the baby weeks before the birth. With great accuracy and confidence the doctors can inform the curious parents how to complete the nursery décor, newborn's wardrobe, and name selection.

The baby's name is chosen with the utmost care. All factors play a part—relatives' expectations, past acquaintances, personal preferences, and the name's meaning. With that decision finalized, this eagerly awaited life takes on identity. Our name soon becomes very important to us. Someone's remembering our name gives us a sense of value. But all that significance must be revealed in just a few words since most of us have just three or four names that identify who we are.

This, however, is not true about God. Throughout the Bible, we learn that He has hundreds of names. Each name reveals a characteristic of God that gives meaning to Who He is. When we learn His names and their meaning, we learn more about our great God. One of His names in the book of Exodus declares His ability to take our weary heart and restore it.

In Exodus 15:22–26, we are introduced to "Jehovah-Rophe." This Hebrew name means "the Lord that heals."[1] When God's people needed His intervention to survive, God revealed this name to Moses. By supplying what they lacked, God laid the groundwork for understanding this restorative process. Let's consider Exodus 15:22–26 to see how God heals and restores.

Over the previous weeks, the children of Israel had seen God work in miraculous ways as His judgment fell on the land of Egypt. With Pharaoh's refusal to release God's people from slavery, God had sent a series of plagues. Pharaoh finally let the children of Israel leave when the tenth affliction took the life of the firstborn in each unprepared house. Moses had led the people across the Red Sea and had delivered them from the Egyptians. Regardless of all that God had done for the Israelites, it was not long before they began to doubt God and complain to Moses.

The traveling nation feared that they had survived the slavery of Egypt only to die in the wilderness. Their anger was directed at Moses, but their grievance was against God. Moses was only God's servant who was chosen to direct their travels. How long could they survive, though, without water? It had already been three days since they had left the shores of the Red Sea. When they arrived at Marah, they found water, but it was undrinkable. The bitter water made the people complain even more.

Moses called upon God for a solution to this crisis. God showed Moses a tree and told him to cast it into the water. When Moses threw the designated tree into the water, God made the water sweet. God's lesson for the people went far beyond the refreshing water. He gave them an enduring promise: "If thou wilt diligently hearken to the voice of the Lord thy God, and wilt do that which is right in his sight, and wilt give ear to his commandments, and keep all his statutes, I will put none of these diseases upon thee, which I have brought upon the Egyptians: for I am the Lord that healeth thee."

Through this precious promise, God revealed His name, Jehovah-Rophe, "the Lord that healeth thee" (Exodus 15:26). God wanted the children of Israel and all mankind to realize that He "would heal, restore, and repair us spiritually and physically—[because] He cares."[2]

God restores us when He gives encouragement and healing to our exhausted spirit.

❋❭❭❭❭ ❋❭❭❭❭ ❋❭ THE SOURCE OF MY RESTORATION ❬❋ ❬❬❬❋ ❬❬❬❬❋

As the tree provided healing for the polluted waters at Marah, God "provided a tree on which the Savior died to heal us of our sins" (John 3:1–21, 31–36).[3] The Lord Jesus heals us through His work on the cross! In Hebrews 12, we are challenged to lay aside the weights and sins that so easily discourage our hearts and hinder our spiritual growth. We must run with patience the pathway of life that the Lord Jesus has given us. But He does not ask us to travel this trail alone. In fact, He knows that we will never endure without His presence: "Looking unto Jesus the author and finisher of our faith; who for the joy that was set before him endured the cross, despising the shame, and is set down at the right hand of the throne of God. For consider him that endured such contradiction of sinners against himself, lest ye be wearied and faint in your minds" (verses 2–3).

We must focus on the finish line where our Savior awaits. He is the author, the originator, and the Creator. He has charted and traveled the path before us. But He is also the finisher. He completed the ministry that God the Father sent Him to earth to accomplish. He is our example that must be followed. He understands all that we face, yet He commands us to not "be wearied and faint in [our] minds." Rather than be discouraged, we must look to Jesus and consider Him, the restorer of our souls: "But thou, O Lord, art a shield for me; my glory, and the lifter up of mine head (Psalm 3:3).

We looked earlier at this entire psalm, which David wrote when he fled from his son Absalom. He was crushed with grief because of his son's insurrection. In the midst of it all, David focused on the Lord. God was his shield of protection and the One Who lifted up his head in the midst of his pain.

I've never been attacked and hunted as David was, but I can identify with the overwhelming weariness that he seemed to be feeling when he wrote this chapter. The cares, temptations, and troubles of this life can easily overtake me when I focus on my circumstances. David clarified his perspective when he declared in verse 3, "But thou, O Lord." All may seem hopeless, but God is there. He is my shield, my defense, and my protection. I can glory and rejoice in Him. He lifts up my weary heart even in the most trying conditions.

Remember when your children were small and you wanted them to look into your eyes? You knew that without focused eye contact, your words of loving reassurance would be missed. What did you do? Did you gently lift that little chin and physically turn his or her gaze toward you? Soon your words of loving comfort took that sad little frown and turned it to a smile. Sometimes the events that brought the tears remained, in spite of your best efforts; but somehow, all seemed better because that sad little heart found comfort in your loving eyes.

This tender picture is what the psalmist wants us to remember. Our Lord lovingly lifts our chin for us to look into His eyes. Why do we resist His corrective, gentle hand? When our focus turns to Him, all is well. The trials may still be dangerously surrounding us, but our heart's cry turns to quiet peace as we gaze into our Savior's face. Let Him be your shield, your protection. Let Him lift your weary, sad face toward Him. May you find Him to be your glory and the lifter up of your head!

The Steps of Restoration

Let's follow the restorative process through the following psalm by noting the changes in the psalmist's heart and attitude from the beginning to the end. The psalmist rejoiced when he turned his eyes upon God and away from his devastating circumstances.

PSALM 77

Verses 1–9

- I cried unto God.
- In trouble, I refused to be comforted.
- I was troubled, complaining, and the Spirit overwhelmed me.
- Is mercy gone?
- Have promises failed?
- Has God forgotten to be gracious?
- Are His mercy and grace taken from me?

But . . .

Verses 10–13

- I will remember!
- I will remember the right hand of the Most High.
- I will remember the wonders of old.
- I will meditate on the work of God.
- I will remember the wonders of God.
- Who is so great as my God?

Verses 14–20

- God does wonders.
- God declares His strength among the people.
- All nature proclaims God's greatness—the waters, clouds, thunder, lightning, and earthquakes.
- God leads His people like a flock.

Our circumstances, trials, and burdens may seem to be unbearable, but God can overcome whatever we face with His matchless grace and power. To receive His glorious victory, we must follow the example of the psalmist and let Him turn our sorrow into songs of praise! The healing may come slowly sometimes, but if we faithfully walk with our Savior, trusting Him to show us each step, we can know the joy of a heart restored. Then we, with the psalmist, can proclaim His greatness.

My Heart Restored

GOD NEVER GIVES US MORE THAN WE CAN HANDLE

Who started this saying? I've heard it my whole life, but the older I get the more I disagree. How can this statement comfort people whose burdens seem to be crushing them? To a mother of nine whose husband unexpectedly dies? To someone facing financial ruin brought on by deception and fraud? To a mother, father, and sister watching their second daughter, her second sister, die slowly from an incurable disease? How can we say this to a community ravaged by yet another hurricane before the damage from the last one is cleaned up? Or to a nation devastated by war and conflict from within and without?

I don't think we can say this truthfully. There are too many things in this life that go beyond my endurance or anyone else's. Yet people seem to successfully face extreme burdens. They go on with their lives, no doubt with grief and sorrow, but still go on. "There hath no temptation taken you but such as is common to man: but God is faithful, who will not suffer you to be tempted above that ye are able; but will with the temptation also make a way to escape, that ye may be able to bear it" (2 Corinthians 10:13).

God is

faithful

I believe there are events that enter our lives that are so devastating that we can survive them only with God's intervention—His gracious help. He provides the extra strength for such times. We quickly find that our resources fail, but His never run dry.

He is faithful and will with every temptation provide the way to escape. He is our gracious, all-powerful God that holds our hand and lovingly guides us through whatever tragedy we face. We have nothing in ourselves for such times; only He has true power and strength. We must totally rest in Him to carry us through whatever our heartbreak, misfortune, or disaster.

What comfort to know that when trials enter our lives we don't have to possess the necessary strength! We don't have to wonder how much more we can endure. We may immediately rest in His all-sufficient grace because

God never gives us more than HE can handle!

Renewed Through His Word

CHAPTER FOUR

We live in a world of communication marvels, surrounded by a multitude of options to keep in touch with those we love. With a tiny phone no bigger than the palm of our hand, we can communicate with anyone around the world by voice, voice messages, text messages, and pictures. With just a click of a computer button, your e-mail message is instantly sent anywhere around the world. Sentence structure, spelling, and punctuation are things of the past as writing rules are abandoned for speed.

The beautiful handwritten correspondence that our grandparents utilized is a lost art. By the time a letter travels from me to you, the news is outdated and irrelevant. The precious time taken to write the letter is considered wasted in the minds of the e-mail generation. These priceless written memories expressed the personality and feelings of the writer with every stroke of the pen.

In spite of all our communication wonders, we live in a society that longs for meaningful relationships. Many around us are searching for direction and fulfillment to their lives. Loneliness is commonplace. Emptiness is a constant. And genuine friendship is beyond the comprehension of most. I wonder how long a society can exist without significant changes occurring.

The hope of mankind is and always has been in the knowledge of God. The Bible is the only place we can find the message of the One Who gives contentment, peace, and unconditional love. The Bible is God's letter of love. Throughout the centuries, it has proven to be the most precious letter anyone could receive. The message is timeless and infallible.

As a pastor's wife, I was daily asked to give direction and guidance to the women in our churches. I knew I did not have the needed answers but was confident that the solution to their problems could be found in God's Word. I had to be a student of the Word to be able to direct the women to the appropriate passages of Scripture. I began to read God's Word with a greater determination to know its content more thoroughly.

My love for the Bible naturally led me to a greater love for the God of the Bible. He alone is the answer to all mankind's needs. It is in His Word that we learn of Him and His loving provision for us. Through diligent study of the Word, He reveals precious truths that help us walk through this life with encouragement and hope.

●〉〉〉 ●〉〉〉 HE RENEWS ME THROUGH HIS WORD 〈〈〈● 〈〈〈●

God, through the prophet Isaiah, compares His Word to the necessary rain that causes plants to grow: "For as the rain cometh down, and the snow from heaven, and returneth not thither, but watereth the earth, and maketh it bring forth and bud, that it may give seed to the sower, and bread to the eater: so shall my word be that goeth forth out of my mouth." He continues, "[My Word] shall not return unto me void, but it shall accomplish that which I please, and it shall prosper in the thing whereto I sent it" (Isaiah 55:10–11).

God's Word should be our first resource when our hearts need revival. Although God reveals Himself in creation, the details of His character are obtained only through His Word. It is within these precious pages that He makes Himself known. Our sinful hearts do not naturally turn to God. We often exhaust our wisdom and solutions before seeking His face. With His Word permeating our heart, we are more likely to look to familiar verses when the wearisome times of discouragement surround us. The Bible portrays itself in many different ways to help us understand all that it can mean to us. No matter what we face or how weary our hearts become, God's Word can be our solace.

- God's Word is my *lamp and light* to show me the way I should go (Psalm 119:105).
- God's Word is the *Word of Life* proclaiming spiritual and eternal life (Philippians 2:16).
- God's Word is my *instruction manual* that teaches me the way I should live (Romans 15:4).
- God's Word is the *mirror of my heart* that reveals what I really am—what God sees me to be (James 1:23–25).
- The apostle Paul referred to the Old Testament as the *oracles, or words, of God* (Romans 3:2).
- In the Christian's armor, the Bible is the *sword of the Spirit*, the only offensive weapon (Ephesians 6:17).
- God's Word is a *continual comfort* for me no matter what I face (1 Thessalonians 4:18).
- The Bible is the *Word of Truth* that never fails (Ephesians 1:13).

~ God's Word is like *nourishment* that helps me grow
(1 Peter 2:2).

In Hebrews 4:12–13, we learn that God's Word is "quick, and powerful, and sharper than any twoedged sword." God's Word is living and dynamic. "It reaches into the inner secrets of man's mind to discern even his **thoughts and intents** . . . God sees man as though he were naked, unable to hide behind excuse or pretense."[1]

●⟩⟩⟩⟩ ●⟩⟩⟩⟩ ●⟩ HE GIVES WORDS OF INSTRUCTION ⟨●⟨⟨⟨● ⟨⟨⟨●

Questions can overwhelm us! Through the Word, God teaches us His will and answers the countless uncertainties of life. In Psalm 32:8, God leaves nothing to speculation when He promises to instruct us in the way He desires for us to walk: "I will instruct thee and teach thee in the way which thou shalt go: I will guide thee with mine eye." He promises to teach and guide us with His eye. When God's Word has priority in our hearts, we will find lessons in righteousness and warning of wrong. Our hearts are renewed when we direct our focus to the education of His Word.

The Word of God should be the focal point of our lives. The apostle Paul says, "Let the word of Christ dwell in you richly in all wisdom; teaching and admonishing one another in psalms and hymns and spiritual songs, singing with grace in your hearts to the Lord" (Colossians 3:16). For His Word to have preeminence, we must be studying the Bible daily and sitting under biblical teaching and preaching. God has designed a special place for us to be taught and encouraged—the local church. When we gather with other believers at a Bible-preaching church, we are giving God and His Word our undivided attention. We can then encourage each other in the Lord as we praise and worship God through the preaching and music.

Are you trying to find the answers to your questions in your own wisdom? It is easy to let the cares and demands of this life keep us from focusing on God and His Word. Our daily time with the Lord can be quickly replaced with the seemingly urgent demands of the moment. What about your church attendance? Other activities can replace our gathering with fellow believers. Maybe you haven't let your attendance wane, but when you are there, a myriad of issues presses against your heart.

As a teacher, it is easy to tell which students are eager to learn. They are the ones focused and concentrating. Their eager faces are a delight to the instructor on any grade level. The contrast is obvious when you compare them to the reluctant learners. The diffident pupil listens with an I-dare-you-to-teach-me-anything attitude. While substituting on the high school level in recent years, I've seen this doubtful look many times. The moment some students enter the room my credentials are under question. Learn from a substitute? Is that possible?

What kind of student of God's Word are you? To truly be taught through the reading and teaching of the Bible, we must submit our heart and life to the Word. We must approach God's Word with an open heart, ready to learn. We must honestly evaluate our life by God's standards. In His Word, we learn Who God is and how He desires to transform us into His image.

Paul wrote to his student Timothy that "all Scripture is given by inspiration of God, and is profitable for doctrine, for reproof, for correction, for instruction in righteousness: that the man of God may be perfect, throughly furnished unto all good works" (2 Timothy 3:16–17). These verses reveal to us the four areas in which we profit as we read and study God's Word. A simple but accurate definition of each word can help us understand these benefits to the fullest.

~ Scripture is profitable for doctrine—what to believe.

~ Scripture is profitable for reproof—what is wrong.

~ Scripture is profitable for correction—how to change.

~ Scripture is profitable for instruction—how to live.

When carefully read and obeyed, God's Word provides all that is necessary to serve for His glory. The lives and situations of the biblical characters show us which paths to follow and which to avoid. Through the actions and choices of those before us, we learn the desires of God's heart. We see the path that will lead a sinner from judgment to blessing. We see Who He is that we may walk in His ways.

HE GIVES WORDS OF ENCOURAGEMENT

Even with the incredible means of communication and the continual contact with scores of people, it is still easy to feel alone. If our world is calm and quiet, the silence can seem deafening as we long for genuine friendship. Through the Word of God, we realize that He never leaves us. He says, "Be strong and of a good courage, fear not, nor be afraid of them: for the Lord thy God, he it is that doth go with thee; he will not fail thee, nor forsake thee. . . . And the Lord, he it is that doth go before thee; he will be with thee, he will not fail thee, neither forsake thee: fear not, neither be dismayed (Deuteronomy 31:6, 8). How encouraging to know that He is always by our side.

Another precious passage on God's continual presence is found in Isaiah 41. In these verses, God calms our fears with the assurance of His help. These verses were a special encouragement to me a few years ago when I faced a health problem: "Fear thou not; for I am with thee: be not dismayed; for I am thy God: I will strengthen thee; yea, I will help thee; yea, I will uphold thee with the right hand of my righteousness. . . . For I the Lord thy God will hold thy right hand, saying unto thee, Fear not; I will help thee (Isaiah 41:10, 13).

The pain had started in the late winter, but I didn't want to admit it to anyone. It was tolerable, so I assumed it would go away. I casually added the issue to the bottom of my list of things to discuss at a routine checkup with my doctor. My appointment had gone very well through the rest of the agenda, so I decided, after a moment's hesitation, to tell my doctor about the lingering pain. Her concern was evident as we discussed the discomfort, so she set a plan in motion to discover its source. After several tests and visits to specialists, the explanation of my pain was still unidentified, but the location was determined. Only surgery could verify the problem.

The surgery was scheduled and my wait began. Although the wait was not unreasonable, the unknown diagnosis loomed over me until the appointed day. The surgery would begin with the simplest approach and then decisions would be made as needed. So even the upcoming solution seemed ominous, as well as unknown.

I repeatedly took my fears to the Lord and went to God's Word to find the comfort and confidence I needed to face so many uncertainties. It was to these verses in Isaiah that my Savior led me. He clearly reminded me that He had me safely in His care. He, my God, would strengthen me and help me through every step of this unknown path. I immediately claimed these verses to be my answer to the fear I faced. He was commanding me to not be afraid because He was with me holding my right hand.

These verses were my hope as I waited for the surgery. They were my comfort as I was prepared for the procedure to begin, and they were my peace as I was rolled into the operating room.

Just before the anesthesia completely put me to sleep, the nurses asked to begin the IV in my left hand. In the midst of my drowsiness I remember thinking, "I'm glad they can do this in my left hand . . . my right hand is busy holding onto my Savior's." But they asked me next for my right hand to do whatever else was needed. I'm sure I hesitated slightly before extending my right hand. No matter what these nurses were doing, I knew He was still holding my hand!

The surgery was far more complicated than the doctor had anticipated. The procedure turned into several hours of work for my physician and of waiting for my family. I spent several days in the hospital and a number of weeks recovering, but the problem had been found and removed. The results could have been far worse. The Lord truly held my hand through it all.

In the weeks that followed, I was often reminded of the Lord's tender love. He never left my side. The recovery days were filled with many hours of sweet fellowship with Him. The stack of books that I read were precious study that He knew I needed for the days ahead. Although most of the books were about Him, there was none I enjoyed more than my Bible.

He gave me the grace to face the fear of the unknown, to endure the pain of the recovery, and to rest the necessary weeks of healing. Through His Word, I found the joy of holding His hand.

❂⟫⟫ ❂⟫⟫ ❂⟫⟫ He Gives Words of Promise ⟨⟨⟨❂ ⟨⟨⟨⟨❂ ⟨⟨⟨⟨❂

From the world's perspective, circumstances can leave us with little hope for tomorrow. The Word gives us the promise, or hope, of heaven. One day, we will stand in His presence! If an eternity in heaven is shaping our outlook, nothing should discourage us. Through God's Word, we are given these precious glimpses of heaven—our future home—and our arrival there. How our hearts should rejoice! Whether our arrival is by death or by the Lord's return, it will be glorious to enter our heavenly home:

> Let not your heart be troubled: ye believe in God, believe also in
> me. In my Father's house are many mansions: if it were not so, I
> would have told you. I go to prepare a place for you. And if I go

and prepare a place for you, I will come again, and receive you unto myself; that where I am, there ye may be also. And whither I go ye know, and the way ye know. Thomas saith unto him, Lord, we know not whither thou goest; and how can we know the way? Jesus saith unto him, I am the way, the truth, and the life: no man cometh unto the Father, but by me. (John 14:1–6)

What about today? We would readily admit that heaven is the glorious and final solution to all our needs, but until that day, how do we endure the current struggles? As I mentioned at the beginning of this chapter, hope for today is found in God's Word. He commands us to not worry about the physical cares of this life. He calls to remembrance that our heavenly Father knows our every need: "Therefore take no thought, saying, What shall we eat? or, What shall we drink? or, Wherewithal shall we be clothed? . . . for your heavenly Father knoweth that ye have need of all these things." If we seek His righteousness first, Jesus will take care of these needs. He says, "Take therefore no thought for the morrow: for the morrow shall take thought for the things of itself" (Matthew 6:31–34).

Many times through the years God has used His Word to remind me that He is my hope. Financial needs can often take my focus from God's sufficiency. I sat at the breakfast table one morning totaling the deposits of our weekly paychecks. Due to unexpected events, the numbers looked scary!

After spending extra time in prayer and Bible reading, I was encouraged. "The Lord is my hope" had been the theme of Romans 15. Verse 13 promises, "The God of hope fill you with all joy and peace in believing, that ye may abound in hope, through the power of the Holy Ghost." He not only promises hope, but He is hope! I prayed asking God to give us encouragement in a way that would unmistakably be from Him. I finished my prayer and Bible reading with a confident peace—He would provide.

A few days before, I had found some money in my husband's sock drawer. He had no idea it was there although it was just inside the drawer and easily seen. We had decided to save this surprise money to buy Christmas gifts. When my husband left for work, I had jokingly said that I was going to go through the sock drawer more thoroughly to see what else I could find.

As I began my cleaning, I went with a smile to my husband's sock drawer. Why not take a closer look? My curiosity wasn't going to be satisfied without further investigation. I began to remove the socks and almost immediately found an envelope with, yes, more money enclosed. I couldn't help but laugh and continue my adventure. The more socks I pulled out the more envelopes I found. Needless to say I emptied that drawer! When I removed the last sock and opened the last card, I was speechless. I added up what I had found. I used the calculator twice to be sure I was accurate— over five hundred dollars! Unbelievable. Some of the envelopes had been tucked away for over eight years. My husband had obviously set aside these gifts and forgotten about them. He probably even thought he had used the contents. But there it was—the provision of God for our present need.

I called my husband and had him guess what I had found. Clearly he had no idea or this nest egg wouldn't have been there. His office setting didn't let him rejoice with a literal shout of joy, but he was thrilled. Together we praised the Lord. My husband reminded me of the time that the Lord provided for Peter's taxes from the mouth of a fish (Matthew 17:24–27). The verses I'd read had assured me of His ability to provide. Our unexpected provision was from an unexpected source—a sock drawer. "But my God shall supply all your need according to his riches in glory by Christ Jesus" (Philippians 4:19).

My Heart Restored

I felt upset without any apparent reason. There wasn't any event of the day that I could blame for this misery. I know feelings are not supposed to control us, but that knowledge didn't seem to relieve my restlessness. It was wrong for my day to have evolved into such a state. After I went to bed that night, I realized what had happened.

Even

our

feeblest

efforts

to honor

God

aggravate

Satan

I had spent the morning working on *My Heart Restored*. I finished the rough draft that would complete the chapters about being renewed through God's Word. It was an incredible joy to see the pages take a form that hopefully would turn a woman's heart to God's Word and ultimately to the God of the Word. Yet I was ending my day struggling with purposelessness. These pages that were meant to refresh the heart of a weary Christian must anger Satan. How he must loathe the possibility of someone finding encouragement in the pages of her Bible. What I had written had incited an attack of doubt and discouragement on my tired soul. The truths of Ephesians 6 tell us that we don't wrestle with flesh and blood. We fight a spiritual battle. Even our feeblest efforts to honor God aggravate Satan. With this realization, an amazing peace flooded my heart. The struggle ended.

I remembered the weeks when I first attempted to put my teaching into writing. My thoughts were bombarded with my inadequacies and ignorance. When I surrendered those doubts and fears to the Lord, He cleared my thoughts and the words started to come. My projects are ultimately His to be used as He sees best. I am simply to share the lessons and blessings He's given me.

May we be true to the path God has for us. May we be saturated with His Word so that our focus never strays from this precious letter. When our hearts are weary, may we immediately go to the Bible, learn of Him, and be encouraged!

Redirected Through His Word

CHAPTER FIVE

We saw in chapter 4 that God's Word answers the questions that plague our weary hearts and gives the encouragement that He is always with us. The Bible also redirects our uncertain steps by helping us see our circumstances from God's point of view. The hope and guidance we find on the pages of Scripture transform times of trial and waiting into seasons of blessing.

HE GIVES WORDS OF GUIDANCE

I am directionally challenged. In spite of my parents both being very gifted with a wonderful sense of direction, I seem to have none. I can read a map well and have successfully navigated for my husband on many vacations through the years. Something is lost, though, when I take that map information and translate it to the real world. Finding my car in a large parking lot has been a trial for years. My children have often come to my rescue when the car seemed to have moved. My greatest comfort in growing older is that satellite-tracking systems are standard equipment for a wireless phone small enough to fit in my purse!

Many times the path of our life also seems unclear. We often find ourselves searching for which direction to go. We might be tempted to say that there are no verses that specifically say, "You should _____." But God's Word is better than a map or GPS guiding us through each day; it has "given unto us all things that pertain unto life and godliness, through the knowledge of him that hath called us to glory and virtue." We can obtain the knowledge of God's will when we receive the "exceeding great and precious promises" of His Word and obediently apply them to our lives (2 Peter 1:3–4). Through the Word, God speaks principles that give us His wisdom and direction. The pathway becomes visible as we seek His will through the guidance of His Word. Our prayer should be as the psalmist prayed in Psalm 25:4, "Shew me thy ways, O Lord; teach me thy paths."

He Gives Words of Grace

There is much in the Bible about waiting on God and how He uses these times in our lives. I have found it is much easier to be busy for the Lord than to be waiting. Waiting is equated with wasting time in the society in which we live. Yet, there are certain lessons that can be comprehended only in the context of inactivity. In the midst of our wait, we can know His peace as the pages of God's Word fill our minds and hearts with the grace to trust Him. God is honored, and we are abundantly blessed when we wait upon Him. That blessing includes knowing God's salvation, goodness, strength, and patience.

God's Word often refers to this waiting process as resting. Restlessness is far more common than resting in our society. Our frustration can be compounded when we see those who reject or ignore

God seeming to prosper. But the Bible says, "Rest in the Lord, and wait patiently for him: fret not thyself because of him who prospereth in his way, because of the man who bringeth wicked devices to pass" (Psalm 37:7).

Have you noticed that we live in a society that expects immediate results? We become far too impatient when things seem unfair, unreasonable, or delayed. We want results yesterday, and to wait for anything is considered only a frustration, not an opportunity to develop patience.

How easy it is to become discouraged when people around us seem to live lives of disobedience to God without apparent consequences. When we strive to be like the Lord Jesus and walk in obedience to Him, the immediate rewards sometimes seem minimal.

The psalmist David reminds us in Psalm 37:1–8 of the peace we can know as we walk with the Lord. This peace is granted only to those who are truly resting in the Lord Jesus and the salvation He provided through His death and resurrection. These guidelines challenge us to trust the Lord for whatever problem we face. Blessings will come at God's appointed time.

Read through the list of directions for sustaining a peaceful heart.

- Psalm 37:1, 7, 8—Don't worry or be envious.
- Psalm 37: 3—Do good.
- Psalm 37: 4—Delight in the Lord.
- Psalm 37: 5—Commit your way to the Lord and trust in Him.
- Psalm 37:7—Rest in Him; wait patiently.
- Psalm 37:8—Stop being angry.

Are you resting in Him today? Take a few minutes to praise God for His control over everything. Thank Him for His Word, which promises the grace to wait for His best. When God seems silent, He is directing us to quietly wait on Him and trust His timing as well as His answers.

❋⟩⟩⟩ ❋⟩⟩⟩ ❋⟩⟩ HE GIVES WORDS OF DEFENSE ⟨⟨⟨❋ ⟨⟨⟨❋ ⟨⟨⟨❋

Do you realize that we are in a spiritual battle? Does the engagement with the enemy drain you of your spiritual strength? You need to claim the verses that teach us what we should do to resist Satan. Satan hates God's Word because it renders him powerless in our lives.

In Ephesians 6:10–20, we are introduced to the armor that God gives us to use when Satan attacks. All the pieces of protection are defensive except for the "sword of the Spirit, which is the Word of God." "The Greek term rendered 'word' is not *logos*, referring to the whole Word of God, but *rhēma*, referring to certain portions or selected verses of Scripture."[1] With that in mind, consider how the following verses can be your response to Satan's temptations or attacks.

Satan's Attack

"You're too tired to go to church and don't need to go like some people do."

> Not forsaking the assembling of ourselves together, as the manner of some is; but exhorting one another: and so much the more, as ye see the day approaching. (Hebrews 10:25)

Application to My Life

"I need to spend time worshiping together with other believers to maintain my walk with the Lord."

Satan's Attack

"You're killing yourself trying to help those people! Nobody cares but you."

And Jesus came and spake unto them, saying, All power is given
unto me in heaven and in earth. Go ye therefore, and teach all
nations, baptizing them in the name of the Father, and of the
Son, and of the Holy Ghost: Teaching them to observe all things
whatsoever I have commanded you: and, lo, I am with you alway,
even unto the end of the world. (Matthew 28:18–20)

Application to My Life

*"My Lord is with me. My ministry is what God has called me to. He
is with me even when I don't see the outward results I wish for. I will
remain faithful. My Lord is faithful to me."*

Satan's Attack

*"I don't think you're going to make it! Look at all you do for God
and He won't even give you the health and strength to do this!"*

It is God that girdeth me with strength, and maketh my way
perfect. (Psalm 18:32)

The Lord will give strength unto his people; the Lord will bless
his people with peace. (Psalm 29:11)

Application to My Life

*"I need to wait on God. He'll renew my strength to continue to love
and serve Him."*

Looking for encouragement at those times of weariness? The
Bible should be the first tool we reach for when we need restoration!
God's Word gives us the instruction, encouragement, promises,
guidance, grace, and defense necessary to know the restful peace of
God that will quiet our overwhelmed souls. His Word is a letter of
love from the dearest friend we could have. In this world of instant
communication, nothing will ever take the place of our heavenly
Father's Word. We must pick it up, read it, and apply it to our hearts
and lives. We can be renewed through His precious Word!

A Woman's Time with God

I have never had a woman tell me that she had too much time! I've heard plenty about too much laundry, too many chores, too many problems, but never too much time. Our days are full of events, planned and unforeseen, that dictate our actions. Little lives need nurturing and care! As a mother of three, I remember how tricky it was to get a shower and to do basic household chores. It's not easy for a woman to read and meditate on God's Word; yet it is through spending time in His Word that we gain the spiritual strength necessary to be godly. Let's consider how to wisely use our time with God.

How Do I Schedule Time in God's Word?

Maintain Realistic Expectations

For a woman no two days are alike. The order that characterized your life vanished with your first job or your first child. The key is to use today's time wisely. Don't expect hours of quiet reading, but use the time you have to learn one truth from God's Word.

Adjust Your Schedule

It's difficult to schedule minutes that don't seem to exist. You may find that you need to eliminate some things from your schedule. What personal or recreational activities could you adjust to have time to spend with your Savior? I know we hesitate to modify the few things we do for fun, but we must be willing to make God our priority. The time you give to Him has eternal benefits.

Make the Time a Habit

Bible study needs to be a part of every day. Experts say it takes three to four weeks of consistently doing an activity for it to become a habit. Try linking your Bible study immediately before or after another activity that you always do—fixing your hair, putting on makeup, showering. Don't let a day go by without spending time with God. At the end of a few weeks of faithful study, you will be amazed at how special this time has become.

SET TIME LIMITS

I accomplish the most when I follow a "to do" list with a designated time limit for each task. Put your time with God at the top of your list and don't let yourself start other necessary duties before spending time with Him. The rest of your responsibilities will go much better if you have put God first.

DESIGNATE A PLACE

Another idea for scheduling time in God's Word is to have a designated spot to sit. Having all your tools in place—study Bible, notebook, dictionary, pen—helps you efficiently spend the time. A friend's special place was a particular chair by a small table where she would sit to read her Bible. When she finished, she would tuck her things under the long tablecloth that covered the little table. Her study materials were handy and her room was neat!

When those few quiet minutes surprise you with their arrival, it is imperative that you be ready—they may not last long! Begin with prayer asking the Lord to quickly quiet your heart and help you think on Him and His Word. Ask Him to show you something about Who He is and what He desires. Thank Him for the time and truths He is about to give you. But now another question arises.

How Do I Remember What I've Read?

WRITE IT DOWN

When you have found that treasure from God's Word, write it down or it will be forgotten ten minutes after you close your Bible! I suggest writing the chosen verse(s) in a daily journal to give you a written record of what you have learned. Be sure to include the date and the reference for the passage you read. This method focuses your attention and documents your blessings for reviewing another day.

MEDITATE ON IT

Do you know how to worry? Then you know how to meditate! Meditate simply means to contemplate, mull over, consider, or turn over in your mind. Do you think about God and His Word throughout your day? Is God a part of your life only when you want Him to be? For the Word to give us the calming rest our hearts desperately need, we must learn to make it our focus throughout our day. "Thou wilt keep him in perfect peace, whose mind is stayed on thee: because he trusteth in thee" (Isaiah 26:3). Wherever we are reading, Old or New Testament, God is proclaimed! His character, His love, His holiness, and His glorious names are revealed to us.

What would you do for peace of mind on any given day? There are so many distractions and burdens that come to rob us of God's peace. We must not let the cares of this life redirect our focus. The secret to a peaceful heart is to be focused on the Lord. And that focus can come only as we meditate on His Word and make Him the master of our lives. God alone is our source of comfort, joy, patience, love, and endurance. We will realize Who He is as we read and meditate on His Word. Don't try to go through your day without spending time with Him! Let thoughts of Him and truths of His Word accompany you throughout each day.

You may want to write the special verse(s) for the day on index cards. If you post the cards in strategic spots around your house, they will remind you to meditate on the treasures you read. When you discover another truth, place the previous card on a ring or in an envelope. Memorize and review these verses when you need refreshed!

Deuteronomy 6:6–7 challenges us to place God's Word before the eyes of children: "These words, which I command thee this day, shall be in thine heart: and thou shalt teach them diligently unto thy children, and shalt talk of them when thou sittest in thine house, and when thou walkest by the way, and when thou liest down, and when thou risest up." Women need these encouraging reminders as much as children. When you see God's Word, you are reminded to keep His truths the continual focus of your heart. With God's promises your central thought, you can effectively share them with others.

APPLY IT

Finding these truths is pointless if you don't apply them in your life. Application is determining how these truths will affect you today. To merely read is not enough; the truths must change your heart. God's Word does not mean one thing to one person and something else to another. However, how you apply the verses may be different in light of your circumstance. For example, mothers with toddlers will find verses on strength to give them hope as they rescue that little one from mischief for the hundredth time. Another mother needs strength to stay a step ahead of an ever-searching teenager. The key is taking Bible truths and allowing them to impact your actions. Reading, surrendering, and applying brings Christlike change—not just academic knowledge.

My Heart Restored

One autumn a few years ago illustrated clearly how God uses His Word to answer my dilemmas. After the first day of teaching for the new school year, my voice seemed weak. Even after a weekend, I knew that something was not working correctly. The doctor diagnosed my problem as asthma; instead of getting better I became worse. A week later she updated her diagnosis to pneumonia after looking at my chest x-rays. The doctor's orders included additional medicine and complete bed rest. October became weeks of solitude with all planned activities and work coming to an abrupt halt.

The most difficult effect was to be at home and too sick to do the work that I dearly love—my writing. To sit at the computer and type was beyond my strength. I felt like I was wasting precious opportunity! But I couldn't muster the strength for what I longed to do. My impatience soared with the approach of November. I was scheduled to speak at a women's seminar in northeastern Pennsylvania. I could barely breathe! How could I speak?

Sleep was difficult. I felt anxious when I lay down to rest. It was so much work to breathe that I felt I needed to stay awake to continue this vital activity. One particular night I went to the pages of my Bible to see what God had to say about these now difficult but essential tasks of breathing and speaking.

I'm never disappointed when I go to God's Word. The search for the answers to this current dilemma was no exception. The words of John the Baptist, recorded in John 3:29–30, gave me one of the reasons the Lord had set me aside: "He that hath the bride is the bridegroom: but the friend of the bridegroom, which standeth and heareth him rejoiceth greatly because of the bridegroom's voice: this my joy therefore is fulfilled. He must increase, but I must decrease."

It was through this illustration of John's relationship to Jesus that I realized why my voice was gone and my activities so limited. The friend of the bridegroom (the best man) found pleasure in the voice of the groom. My joy was to come from hearing the voice of my Lord. Too often His voice is lost in the noise of my foolish words and thoughts. The doctor said my voice was gone because of the pneumonia. And that was no doubt true. But I realized there was more to it than just a medical answer. My voice was gone so that I might better hear the voice of the bridegroom—the Lord Jesus. My prayer became that of John's, "He must increase, but I must decrease." With the loving care and support of family, friends, and co-workers, I began to improve. God allowed me to speak in Pennsylvania. He knew I needed those weeks aside to be ready to minister to the women who attended.

Are you weary with little quiet time to spend in God's Word? Maybe time with the Lord has seemed impossible to fit into your busy day. Why not try these ideas? When you make God's Word a daily priority, you'll find His wisdom and grace growing you into a woman that brings Him glory.

As We Read Your Holy Word

As I read Your Holy Word,

Help me see, Lord, help me learn.

Holy Spirit, from its pages lead the way.

Come and melt my stubborn will;

Make my heart and soul be still.

As I read Your Word, may I heed it and obey.

Like the first rays of morning light,

it will pierce my darkest night,

Showing sins of doubt and fear within my heart,

Showing self-confidence and pride,

The rebel thoughts that plague my mind.

Then it brings cleansing hope that quiets my heart.

I'm never

disap-

pointed

when

I go to

God's

Word

So as we read Your Holy Word,

Help us see, Lord, help us learn.

Holy Spirit, from its pages lead the way.

Come and melt our stubborn will;

Lord, make our hearts and souls be still.

As we read Your Word, may we heed it and obey.

Open my eyes and let me see

glimpses of truth You have for me,

For in Your Word I find the truth that sets me free.

Fred and Ruth Coleman[2]

Refreshed in His Presence

CHAPTER SIX

Having a cell phone with lots of minutes has taken on new significance now that I'm a grandmother. It's not unusual for me to receive multiple calls a day with news about my granddaughters. These early months are full of things to learn. My daughters know that I want the latest news! So if my little girls have rolled over or cut a tooth or said a new word, I definitely want to be part of the celebration. No matter where I am—at home or on the road—I can usually get the report. However, there are times that my cell phone reception is hindered by my surroundings or I'm teaching a class and the exciting information is left on voice mail to be applauded later.

In spite of the communication marvels of our day, our closest friends and relatives are not available to us twenty-four hours a day, seven days a week. But with God, we always have immediate access to His throne of grace through prayer. No need to wonder if He is away from home, busy with someone else, or wanting time alone.

God's continual presence is promised to us throughout His Word. No matter the time or the day, He is always with us to hear and answer our prayers and to share the joys and trials of this life.

Spiritual weariness can come when we try to live for the Lord without spending meaningful time with Him in prayer. Neglecting to pray forces us to walk in our own strength instead of God's. Often we feel we must have a certain length of time devoted to praying; but when blocks of free time never come, we simply don't pray. According to 1 Thessalonians 5:17, our prayers need to be endless. D. L. Moody was quoted as saying, "I never pray longer than five minutes; but I never go more than five minutes without praying."[1] Our prayers should naturally fall from our lips in continual fellowship with our Lord. While going about the routine of our day, our thoughts should allow us to share all we encounter with our Savior.

We also need the discipline of praying. Prayer is an exercise that challenges our focus; we are speaking to God, Whom we cannot see. To spend time in prayer requires concentration and focus. We will want to extend our time of focused prayer to longer segments as we exercise and build the discipline it requires.

The refreshing that our hearts long for comes from talking to our heavenly Father in prayer. When we know God as our Savior and friend, the time we spend in prayer will comfort and encourage us. Daily time in prayer is crucial in developing this personal relationship with God. He is glorified when we come to Him with our needs, our sorrows, our longings, and our praise.

He Gives Refreshment to Continue

Let's first consider the example of the Lord Jesus. "Jesus pulled away from people, even from his close friends, because He knew of the power available in the presence of the Father."[2] If Jesus needed this communion with God the Father, how much greater is our need?

In Matthew 14:15–21, we have the account of Jesus feeding the five thousand men and their families. This incredible event immediately preceded one of Jesus' times in prayer with God the Father. The multitudes had been with Jesus all day. Many of their sick had been healed, and all had been impacted by the words Jesus spoke. When the day drew to a close, the disciples realized that the people had gone for hours with no food. The disciples recommended sending the people back to their villages, but Jesus' solution was to feed them. It was Philip who quickly did the math and announced that even a day's wage would not begin to sufficiently feed so many. Where would the disciples find such an amount? The only food available was a small boy's simple lunch of five loaves and two fish.

Jesus told the disciples to have the families sit down in groups of fifty. With eyes gazing toward heaven, Jesus blessed the meager provisions and began to break the bread and fish into pieces. When the baskets were ready, the disciples passed them around. Matthew 14:20 states, "And they did all eat, and were filled: and they took up of the fragments that remained twelve baskets full." Not only had everyone been served, but twelve baskets of leftovers were collected. Jesus had provided in abundance!

Such a demonstration left the people, including the disciples, amazed. After sending the disciples out in the ship to meet Him on the other side of the sea, Jesus sent the multitude back to their homes. Jesus then retreated to the mountains for a time of solitude and prayer. While Jesus was in prayer, the disciples faced a terrifying storm in the middle of the sea.

Through the spray of the monstrous waves, the apostles saw the figure of a man approaching the ship. The disciples were gripped with fear as this ghostlike shape came closer. When Jesus heard their cries, He spoke to them above the howl of the storm: "Be of good cheer; it is I, be not afraid" (Matthew 14:27). It was Peter who tested the Lord's words and bravely stepped from the boat to walk on the water to Jesus. After just a few steps, the storm drew Peter's attention away from the Lord. Peter's faith was briefly demonstrated in this astonishing act. Once Jesus and Peter were safely in the boat, the storm ended.

What is significant about Jesus' time alone in prayer coming between outstanding moments of public ministry? Jesus needed continuing power to maintain His service. Since He suffered with the nonsinful aspects of the human body, He was tired after the first event and needed rest and communion with God the Father before the next. It was through solitude in the presence of God the Father that He found the rest He needed.

Jesus trained the apostles to follow His example. In Mark 6, Jesus sent the disciples out in groups of two to minister. They preached, cast out devils, and healed the sick. Jesus welcomed the disciples back and eagerly listened to them share the details of their missionary trip. After this intense ministry, Jesus instructed His weary friends to go to a deserted place to rest. When the disciples returned from this time of respite, they helped with the feeding of the five thousand.

Jesus gives us an example that we cannot minimize. Jesus maintained His strength during His years of ministry through times of quiet surrender. He also recommended rest for His disciples after their time away preaching. Why with such clear instruction do we neglect our prayer time and try to continually serve Him in our own strength?

He Gives Confidence in His Sovereignty

God refreshes our insecure hearts when we go to Him in prayer acknowledging His sovereignty and providence. Sovereignty is God's "absolute independence to do as He pleases and His absolute control over the action of all His creatures. No creature, person, or empire can either thwart His will or act outside the bounds of his will."[3] Providence is God's foreseeing and supplying through His "continuous activity . . . in His creation by which He preserves and governs."[4] He continually orchestrates the events to accomplish His purposes.

When we are trusting in God's sovereignty and providence, we take our problems to Him and let Him show us the answers. We recognize that nothing touches our lives without the permission of our loving heavenly Father. He is the supreme ruler over all. We can be confident that He will do what is best.

Throughout the Bible, we learn that God thoroughly understands the issues of daily life and of divine truth. He appreciates the constant struggles and problems we face, but He also has supreme authority in all areas. No matter how profound or how simple the issues are, God is in control. He gives us what is best to accomplish His will and proclaim His glory.

Far too often our outlook is not God's. We see the trials of this life as interrupting our happiness. Yet when we go to God in prayer, we find reassurance that His sovereign will is being accomplished. Our holiness is being developed as He sees best. When we pray, we need to acknowledge His sovereignty and surrender to His insight and wisdom.

Far too often we see our lives as single events that randomly come and go without connection. Only in retrospect can we fit the pieces together to get a glimpse of how they relate. This whole process reminds me of doing a puzzle. When our children were young, they enjoyed the wooden puzzles with a few simple shapes fitting together to make a picture. As the children grew, so did the complexity of the puzzles.

By the time they were early teens, they took on the challenge of puzzles with hundreds of pieces. Somewhere between the wooden pieces and the hundreds of pieces, they lost me. Their father loved the harder ones, so it became a special time for him and our children to share. On occasion, I would offer to help, but after they caught me placing pieces together that didn't fit, I was relegated to the sidelines. My role as encourager was more to my liking anyway. My amazement was genuine when they put that last piece in place and I captured the moment with the camera. Those scores of tiny pieces when fit together properly revealed a picture—a picture beyond my ability to imagine from a box full of arbitrary shapes.

God in His sovereignty knows the finished picture of our lives. Each event that seems so random is a piece in our life-puzzle. Because He knows our finished image, He knows how each piece must be placed and the order that it must be added. He knows the beautiful picture we will be when we stand in His presence. We can take our burdens to Him in prayer and rest confidently that He will fit the pieces of our lives together as He sees best. Oh, that we would trust His sovereign wisdom.

●≫≫≫ He Gives Relief When I Surrender My Burdens ≪≪≪●

Some tasks are simply beyond my strength. One such task was lifting my son's book bag. He often found it easier to drop the bag at the first possible location inside the back door. Sometimes he was back out the door to work or the next activity without my noticing and reminding him to move this obstacle. There were days when it could not remain in this spot until he returned home; I had to move it. This was not an easy task. Even with the incredible strength that his weightlifting activities had given him, how did he lug it around all day? My best option for moving it from here to there was to drag it across the floor to the desired location.

This is often the way we pray. We know we should take our burdens to the Lord and leave them at His feet. These encumbrances weigh heavy on our hearts, and we long for relief from carrying them. We know God's Word clearly tells us to give our cares to

Him because He cares for us. We lay our troubles before Him; but, when we say "Amen," we drag them away with us—a heavier load than when we started. Don't pray and hang on. God gives great relief when we surrender our burdens to Him in prayer. The apostle Peter said, "Casting all your care upon him; for he careth for you" (1 Peter 5:7). The psalmist admonished, "Cast thy burden upon the Lord and he shall sustain thee: he shall never [permit] the righteous to be [shaken]" (Psalm 55:22).

I sometimes feel as though I must carry the burdens of every-one I know. My load is light compared to many, but I still become overwhelmed with the diversity of issues I feel responsible to help solve. When I sat down with my cup of tea one morning, I eagerly opened my Bible anticipating a solution for the weight that seemed heavy on my heart.

I opened to 2 Kings 3, where I'd ended the day before. This chapter is in the middle of God's miracles through His prophet Elisha. That's what I needed—a miracle. What a fascinating account of God's provision. Under Elisha's direction the people dug ditches for God to fill with the necessary water for the Israelites and their livestock. When the ditches were dug, the people's part was com-plete. God had to do the rest. The people had to step back; they had no way to fill these trenches.

How hard it must have been for the Israelites to rest that night with their helplessness engulfing them. It was up to God to provide. How often I am there. My frantic efforts crash into the wall of my inadequacy! I can do no more—only pray, step back, and watch God work. When the Israelites awoke the next morning, the bless-ing of God awaited them. The ditches were full of water. God had quietly filled them as the people slept. Elisha's words in verse 18 put everything in perspective: "And this is but a light thing in the sight of the Lord: he will deliver the Moabites also into your hand."

This verse declares the solution to our load of care. No matter the weight of all our problems stacked one upon the other, our burden is a light thing for the Lord. To us, our burden will always be heavy; to Him it will ever be light. Will everything be solved immediately? No, but the promises are there. He can and will carry every burden we give to Him. We must do as the children of Israel did—pray, step back, and watch God work.

What burdens in your life do you pick back up after you pray about them?

We all have certain areas that seem to trouble us. Write each of these burdens on an index card. Take these cards to the place where you spend time praying and pray about each one. When you finish, leave the stack of cards at this spot. Don't take the cards with you. If you find yourself worrying over any of these concerns, go back, pray again, and ask the Lord to help you trust the burden to Him. Give the request to God again by leaving the card at your place of prayer. Follow the words to the old gospel song "Sweet Hour of Prayer."

> Sweet hour of prayer! Sweet hour of prayer!
> Thy wings shall my petition bear
> To Him whose truth and faithfulness
> Engage the waiting soul to bless;
> And since He bids me seek His face,
> Believe His Word and trust His grace,
> I'll cast on Him my ev'ry care,
> And wait for thee, sweet hour of prayer.
>
> William B. Bradbury[5]

He Gives Peace As I Accept His Answers

Many people miss the peace of God simply because they will not accept the answers to prayer God gives them. They have not only taken their problems to the Lord, but they have taken their solutions to Him too. Many believe that their prayer must include the answer, how God should respond. Is there only one possible, right answer? "For my thoughts are not your thoughts, neither are your ways my ways, saith the Lord. For as the heavens are higher than the earth, so are my ways higher than your ways, and my thoughts than your thoughts" (Isaiah 55:8–9). If God's ways are not our ways, who are we to declare the responses that God must give? The peace that our weary soul desires may come simply by accepting the answers that God gives, even if they are not what we would have chosen.

How do you respond when God gives solutions different from what you planned? When God answers unexpectedly, do you struggle? We should give our problems to Him, surrender our pre-determined solutions, and let Him provide the outcome. We do not have to wonder if God's answers are right. God makes no mistakes. His ways are always best.

God delights in giving us the desires of our hearts. But in His wisdom, He withholds what we long for if it is not good for us. We need to accept and rest in Him. With that acceptance, He'll give peace. Too often we simply do not know God well enough to realize His desires and recognize His will. As we read His Word and learn of Him, we will learn to surrender our desires gladly, trust God's answers unreservedly, and know His peace completely.

He Gives Grace to Trust His Silence

God's answers come in different forms. A yes or no gives clarity for tomorrow—we will either proceed with our current option or turn to approved alternatives. Sometimes our questions are answered by God's silence. Time stands still as we wait for God's solution. The silence of the wait constantly reverberates that nothing is settled, nothing is clear. We do not know which step is right; therefore, to remain constant is our only option. We would much rather be busy or at least think that God is busy. Waiting requires sitting at the feet of our Savior and exchanging our timetable for His.

The anguish of relentless silence is one of God's tools to grow us in His grace. Through the grace of God, we can trust Him in times of uncertainty. The gracious silence demands that we ask ourselves if we love God or if we love His gifts and His works? Do we question His love for us? These quiet times reveal the scope of His grace. His grace, His enabling power, keeps us from questioning His love and goodness in times of silence.

These times of waiting were familiar to the Hebrew people as they wandered through the wilderness. Moses and the people never knew how long they would be camped at any location. The pillar of cloud during the day and of fire at night signaled their travel instructions. If the cloud moved, they moved; if the cloud rested, they rested. Their entire existence was waiting to get ready to move. These seemingly unproductive days were used by God to grow His people. Their faith grew by remembering the past:

> And thou shalt remember all the way which the Lord thy God led thee these forty years in the wilderness, to humble thee, and to prove thee, to know what was in thine heart, whether thou wouldst keep his commandments, or no. And he humbled thee, and suffered thee to hunger, and fed thee with manna . . . that he might make thee know that man doth not live by bread only, but by every word that proceedeth out of the mouth of the Lord doth man live. (Deuteronomy 8:2–3)

Remembering is not as easy as it once was. My memory can be clouded with so many present issues that yesterday seems lost. I have especially noticed fogginess in the days of my own wilderness waiting. Cares and responsibilities often swirl around me with such confusion that to reach a conclusion in any area is difficult.

These verses in Deuteronomy challenge us to remember all the ways that God cares for us and grows us in the midst of our wilderness. He wants us to realize that these are not wasted days. This waiting is important to our growing "in grace and in the knowledge of our Lord and Saviour" (2 Peter 3:18). We must walk faithfully in the steps He has ordained.

He gives us reasons in Deuteronomy for the seasons of silence we often face, reasons we must stay focused upon if we are to understand the purpose for this journey. Our wilderness will be wasted if we do not remember the precious lessons that He is trying to teach us.

GOD'S PURPOSE FOR MY WILDERNESS OF WAITING

- To humble me (Deuteronomy 8:2, 3, 16)
- To reveal my heart (Deuteronomy 8:2, 16)
- To test my obedience (Deuteronomy 8:2)
- To order my priorities (Deuteronomy 8:3)
- To mold me into His likeness (Deuteronomy 8:16)

It is essential in these times of waiting on God that we continue to pray without ceasing. Too often we respond to God's silence with a silence of our own. God desires that we continue to faithfully bring our burdens and questions to Him in prayer, trusting Him to hear and answer in His perfect timing and way. Thank God for the times of silence. Remember His lessons from the past. Ask Him to give you the grace to praise Him for the answers He'll one day reveal.

HE GIVES OPPORTUNITY TO GIVE THANKS IN EVERYTHING

How often do we stop to thank God for all He has done for us? We are a people who quickly forget the blessings God has given. The praise that we should offer can be eclipsed by circumstances that quickly surround us. First Thessalonians 5:17 states, "Pray without ceasing." A continual spirit of prayer from a heart of praise leads to endless thanksgiving even in the middle of trials.

Our praise should be for all that God in His wisdom and sovereignty sends to us. Prayer should be our expression of praise and thanks to God. Do you thank God for your circumstances? Can you thank God before He answers, or do you wait to see if you like His responses before you thank Him?

Since we are so prone to complain and see the negative in a situation, we must discipline ourselves to praise God for everything. We must make a conscious effort to set aside what comes naturally—selfishness, complaining, stubbornness, and pride—and offer our praise as a sacrifice to God. Paul says in 1 Thessalonians 5:18, "In every thing give thanks: for this is the will of God in Christ Jesus concerning you."

Why do we still struggle in this area? We have head knowledge of this concept, but our hearts have trouble catching up and maintaining this thankful acceptance of all things. It's easy to be thankful for the beautifully wrapped packages that come our way in the form of blessings. It's the plain and unattractive, even painful, events that make being thankful beyond our strength. It is at those times that we must claim His matchless grace and offer Him a sacrifice of praise. Everything that touches our life is from His hand—in His will. May we praise Him for everything. May we accept everything as His will. May we do what is right and praise Him for whatever He sends our way. Whatever touches us is from His perfect, loving hand. If praising God in prayer is a habit, we will rejoice even when our burdens are great.

How would you describe your prayer life? When you pray, do you find the refreshing restoration that your heart needs? Realize that when you go to God in prayer you are entering into His presence. Be ready to cast your burdens and requests at His feet and leave them there. Be willing to accept whatever answers He sends. Remember that His ways are not your ways, but His ways are always best. Determine to spend time in prayer today and in the days ahead. When your heart is weary, keep praying!

My Heart Restored

Some of my husband's and my dearest friends have a beautiful cabin on a Canadian lake. On several occasions, while our children were young, they invited our family to join them at this beautiful vacation spot. This remote haven is unlike the tourist spots that have become so overcrowded here in the States. In fact, on our first several visits with them, there was no road to the cabin. We would park our car in a cove and they would take our luggage and us by boat to the cabin. The beauty of this isolated spot was beyond description.

Refreshing will come when we go to God in prayer

When our children were elementary school ages, the action was constant. The daily activities usually included a fishing expedition with a delicious catch. On one fathers-and-children outing, the results were quite comical. Since there were more children than fathers, the adventure was a constant call for help. Between tangled lines, hooks caught in trees, and an occasional fish, the dads didn't have time to catch their breath.

But the climax came with the most vigorous cast of the day. Not only were the bait, line, and bobber cast into the water, so was the rod and reel. There was quite a scramble as the dads did a variety of elaborate maneuvers to retrieve the overextended throw. What a sight it was to see the circus of fishermen. And

the grand finale—one dad jumping in! The kids had a great time. The dads were ready for a nap.

Although it was inappropriate for the little fisherman to throw in the rod and reel, this is not unlike what our praying should be. When we are told to cast all our care upon Him, this is what comes to my mind. I am sure we often cast our requests before Him but keep a firm grip on the controls—the rod and reel. Oh, that we would let go and surrender to God's rule of our lives. Refreshing will come when we go to God in prayer and cast all our cares at His feet—hook, line, sinker, and rod and reel.

Resting in
His Grace

CHAPTER SEVEN

I could understand why my daughter, although not an avid dog
lover, had fallen for this lost dog. His big dark eyes soften your heart
immediately. The tilt of his head reveals his playful personality. The
joyful wag of his almost-too-long tail exposes his comical, mischie-
vous heart. His silky coat makes petting him irresistible. And I sup-
pose all of this had made his visit to our house an easy decision.
My son-in-law had reseeded the grass in the backyard of their new
home, and somehow mixing Hudson with freshly seeded grass was
not in the realm of reality. So Hudson came to our backyard to give
the new sprouts a fighting chance.

The neighbors' dogs immediately greeted Hudson. On one side
live two dogs, Tinkerbell and Ariel. Since they have each other, they
felt obligated to acknowledge Hudson's presence with their finest
barking. But on the other side, Sadie lives alone with only an occasional time of play with her busy owners. She welcomed Hudson

with a totally different approach from the neighboring counterparts. Her barks were just as loud, but reverberated with tones of pure delight. She was thrilled to have such a handsome neighbor.

They contented themselves for the first few days with races up and down the fence row. It was impressive to see the speed and grace with which these two dogs raced. The competition soon went from a friendly contest to a true friendship. No longer was it enough to communicate through the chainlink fence. The desire to be on the same side became more than Sadie could deal with. Hudson did not directly participate in Sadie's plan for escape, but it was clear that he was enticing Sadie to our yard—the greener grasses.

I hated to see Hudson go. But the holes under the fence by the insistent neighbor canine gave us all no choice. Sadie became obsessed with being in our yard with Hudson. The first hole was followed by the next and then the next. She could dig the new one faster than we could fill the previous. There was no stopping her. The fence could not hold her. The wood, cement blocks, and tent stakes couldn't fill in the gaps sufficiently to keep her from digging her way to friendship. So Hudson went back home, sadly limited to the deck until the grass took root. He was given extra walks and attention, but he desperately missed Sadie. I'm sure he soon forgot his new but brief friendship, but he did seem sad (or maybe just exhausted after his week of wild play).

This whole account was fresh on my mind as I taught a lesson on resting in God's grace. Sadie's determination is like my own at times. I too can be dogged in my pursuits. I struggle to solve the needs at hand in my own way and not rest in God's perfect grace. I labor to circumvent a problem or to attain what I desire instead of waiting on the gracious hand of my heavenly Father, Who knows best. Although He lovingly brings me back to His side, I often plunge ahead, digging out a solution not so different from my last feeble attempt.

God longs for us to resign our will to His. He extends to us His gracious solution to our every need. He offers His all-knowing, all-wise answers to our questions. Oh, that we would rest in His amazing grace, stop our futile attempts to run our lives, and surrender to the boundaries He lovingly places around us. God wants to bless and protect us!

We ended our last chapter with the challenge to praise God in prayer. Our hearts are encouraged when we consider all the Lord has done for us. Our times of prayer should be sweet communication with our loving heavenly Father. Thanking Him for all He's done, casting our burdens at His feet, and asking Him for wisdom should all be a part of our time in prayer. What answers, blessings and encouragements has the Lord given you as a result of your time in His presence?

Hebrews 4:16 says, "Let us therefore come boldly unto the throne of grace, that we may obtain mercy, and find grace to help in time of need." You may have heard prayer referred to as the "throne of grace." This expression is often used without understanding its full meaning and significance. We may be able to picture prayer as approaching God's throne and making requests before Him. But where does grace fit in? To walk in the grace of God will give us peace even in the midst of great trials. God freely offers us His grace and with His grace comes rest.

He gives me rest when I allow Him to minister His grace to me and to make me an instrument of grace to others.

What Is Grace?

We must understand grace to rest in it. *Grace* is a word frequently used in spiritual conversation; yet if asked to define it, few could give a clear and practical definition. We must comprehend the meaning to appreciate this precious word. Consider the following definitions of grace from some well-known authors:

"God's unmerited favor to us through Christ whereby salvation and all other blessings are freely given to us . . . God's grace . . . [is] the source of all blessings."[1]

"God's divine assistance to us through the Holy Spirit . . . God's grace expressed specifically as the work of the Holy Spirit within us."[2]

"The grace of God in the New Testament is His unmerited favor in the gift of His Son, who offers salvation to all and who gives to those who receive Him as their personal Saviour added grace for this life and hope for the future."[3]

"Grace is the favor of God in giving His Son and the benefit to men of receiving that Son."[4]

"God's grace is more than a pardon; it is a constant, ever-flowing *provision*, a reassuring *presence*, and an incredible *power*."[5]

The Old Testament alludes to grace when it refers to the undeserved favor God bestows on mankind. It is vividly depicted in the steadfastness of several Old Testament saints. Redemption and grace are only partially revealed through the ceremonies and laws that God designed for Israel to observe and obey. Jesus' death, burial, and resurrection fulfill the Old Testament ceremonies, and the New Testament reveals the Lord Jesus as the embodiment of grace. Grace was the focus of Christ's mission here on earth. Paul, through inspiration of God, revealed and explained this precious truth in his epistles to the early churches.

To state it simply, grace is God's undeserving and enabling power that saves us and then upholds us as we walk the Christian life and minister to others. When we get a glimpse of God's grace, we can rest and rejoice. We can live each day in confident peace realizing that His grace has given us not only the power to be saved but also the power to walk through this life.

GRACE ILLUSTRATED

We see grace illustrated in Luke 17. In this passage God's grace is shown through the relationship of a servant to his master. Jesus asked the apostles, "Which of you, having a servant plowing or feeding cattle, will say unto him . . . when he is come from the field, Go and sit down to meat? And will not rather say . . . Make ready wherewith I may sup, and . . . serve me, . . . and afterward thou shalt eat . . . ? Doth he thank that servant because he did the things that were commanded him?" He then answered His own question: "I [think] not. So likewise ye, when ye shall have done all those things which are commanded you, say, We are unprofitable servants; we have done that which was our duty to do" (Luke 17:7–10).

From these verses we learn some important facts about grace and our continual need for it. Consider each statement in light of this servant-master relationship.

- "We will always be dependent on grace."
- "We will never work our way . . . out of debt to a place where God is in *our* debt."
- "We can *never* treat God with grace."
- "He . . . always giv[es] us more than what we deserve, and *we* . . . always ow[e] *Him* thanks."
- "God is just as free to bless us *before* we get our act together as He is *after*."[6]

This grace, this power, is found in God alone through all that He is and does. When sin entered the world in the Garden of Eden, God knew that man would never be able to provide for sin's debt. Only through the shed blood of Jesus on the cross would such a debt be satisfied. So God gave to the world what mankind could never earn—a Savior. In that undeserving gift, salvation was extended. After man accepts God's gracious gift of salvation, a life of loving service is possible with God's enabling power—God's grace. Nothing of grace can be earned. If we deserved it, it would not be grace. When we rest in His grace, our actions become acts of love and gratitude done in His strength. Paul says in 2 Corinthians, "And he said unto me, My grace is sufficient for thee: for my strength is made perfect in weakness. Most gladly therefore will I rather glory in my infirmities, that the power of Christ may rest upon me" (12:9). Paul also said in Ephesians 2:7 that God would show us as Christians "the exceeding riches of his grace in his kindness toward us through Christ Jesus."

HE GIVES GRACE TO MATCH MY EVERY NEED

MY NEED FOR SALVATION

When we understand God's grace, we can quit struggling to earn and maintain our salvation. God accomplished it all. There is nothing left for us to do but simply receive it. His grace provides our greatest need—a Savior. His gracious gift of salvation is always extended. To stand before Him in righteousness, we simply claim what Jesus did on the cross in our place.

Jerry Bridges explains it this way in his book *Transforming Grace*: "Grace is God's free and unmerited favor shown to guilty sinners who deserve only judgment. It is the love of God shown to the unlovely. It is God reaching downward to people who are in rebellion against Him."[7] When we are saved by grace through faith in Jesus, we are made alive! We were dead in our sins, but by the power or grace of God, we are made alive in Him. In Ephesians 2:1–10, we learn what this power of God has accomplished in us through His gracious plan of salvation.

Our sin is pictured in Ephesians 2:1–3.

> And you hath he quickened, who were dead in trespasses and
> sins; wherein in time past ye walked according to the course of
> this world, according to the prince of the power of the air, the
> spirit that now worketh in the children of disobedience: among
> whom also we all had our conversation in times past in the lusts

of our flesh, fulfilling the desires of the flesh and of the mind; and were by nature the children of wrath, even as others.

In our sinful state we

- were spiritually dead in our sins (verse 1).
- lived only for this world and obeyed Satan (verse 2).
- lived to fulfill our selfish, sinful desires and thoughts (verse 3).

In verses 4–6, the phrase "but God" shows that God's answer to our sin is love! "But God, who is rich in mercy, for his great love wherewith he loved us, even when we were dead in sins, hath quickened us together with Christ, (by grace ye are saved;) and hath raised us up together, and made us sit together in heavenly places in Christ Jesus."

Through His divine love God gives

- spiritual life (verse 5).
- new life (verse 6).
- a new relationship with Him (verse 6).

In verses 7–10, we learn of the purpose for God's saving grace.

That in the ages to come he might shew the exceeding riches of his grace in his kindness toward us through Christ Jesus. For by grace are ye saved through faith; and that not of yourselves: it is the gift of God: not of works, lest any man should boast. For we are his workmanship, created in Christ Jesus unto good works, which God hath before ordained that we should walk in them.

God gives us grace to

- save us (verse 8).
- stop us from boasting in our own works (verse 9).
- make us into His image (verse 10).
- do good works now that we are saved (verse 10).

MY NEED FOR SPIRITUAL GROWTH

As Paul reveals and explains grace, we realize Christians mature by the grace of God. Grace is "God's divine assistance to us through the Holy Spirit."[8] We can quit struggling to become like Christ in our strength. He accomplished it all for us on the cross. His grace is sufficient for both saving and maturing us. When we spend time in the Word and in prayer, the Holy Spirit is within us to guide and instruct us. Through His gracious assistance, we gain an understanding of God and His will for our lives. Our desire to obey Him and be like Him will grow as we daily seek to know Him: "But grow in grace, and in the knowledge of our Lord and Saviour Jesus Christ" (2 Peter 3:18).

Jerry Bridges states,

> Growing in grace is most often used to indicate growth in Christian character.... [A] more accurate meaning is to continually grow in our understanding of God's grace, especially as it applies to us personally, to become progressively more aware of our own continued spiritual bankruptcy and the unmerited, unearned favor of God.[9]

As we grow in our understanding of grace, we cannot help but grow closer to our Lord.

MY NEED FOR THE TRIALS OF THIS LIFE

God's grace matches our every need. He provides the power that we need to endure whatever we face. Even in our weaknesses, we can be strong when we rely on His might and not our own. When events or trials in our lives seem abundant and beyond our ability to endure, He gives us grace to sustain us.

His grace is immeasurable and immediate. "For daily needs there is daily grace; for sudden needs, sudden grace; for overwhelming need, overwhelming grace. God's grace is given wonderfully, but not wastefully; freely but not foolishly; bountifully but not blindly."[10] No matter how great or small the need may be, His grace matches. Whatever our burden, His grace is sufficient!

For a few years I worked as a dental assistant. The first months were not easy as I endeavored to learn the routines of the many procedures the dentist performed. Every case would offer new challenges even if the basic restorations were common. I labored diligently to master the techniques required and prided myself in being able to anticipate the doctor's needs. After years of working together, I became proficient in anticipating the next step and would have what the dentist needed ready and waiting. On many occasions when he would ask for an instrument or material, I would already have the object in my hand waiting for him to take it. He would merely smile and slightly shake his head—a complimentary gesture that let me know he was amazed at my forethought.

When I think of these dental scenarios, I think of God's grace. But with our heavenly Father, His gracious hand is always extended. When we explain to Him our trials, He already knows and is lovingly extending the grace to meet what our heart requires. Whether it is His forgiveness, His strength, His comfort, or His provision, He knows. His greatest desire is for us to reach out and gratefully accept His gracious offer.

I'm so glad He doesn't leave us to our own devices to live the Christian life. He saves and keeps us by His grace. He truly is our all-sufficient, all-knowing, all-powerful God, Who has given us the same promise He gave to Paul. "My grace is sufficient for thee: for my strength is made perfect in weakness" (2 Corinthians 12:9).

Oh, that our response would be like Paul's. "Most gladly therefore will I rather glory in my infirmities, that the power of Christ may rest upon me. Therefore I take pleasure in infirmities, in reproaches, in necessities, in persecutions, in distresses for Christ's sake: for when I am weak, then am I strong" (2 Corinthians 12:9–10).

◉⟩⟩⟩ ◉⟩⟩⟩ HE GIVES GRACE FOR FAITHFUL SERVICE ⟨⟨⟨◉ ⟨⟨⟨◉

I was not always able to anticipate the doctor's next step when he was contemplating the best approach to take. He would sometimes reach out for what he wanted without specifying his decision. At those times, I realized that I couldn't give him what I did not have. The same is true in ministering to others. We cannot give what we don't have!

How can we give to others when our heart feels so empty? This barrenness leaves us drained of the necessary energy to continue helping others. The simplest gesture of caring leaves us exhausted and ineffective. Our ability to encourage others in the Lord is overshadowed by our weakness. We seemingly have nothing to give. We may try to keep pointing others to God, but our attempts lack genuine passion. Our service loses its joy as we struggle to diligently continue. Our reason for ministering—to bring glory to God—is lost.

The apostle Paul clearly understood ministry through grace. Many times throughout his epistles he spoke of serving by God's grace. Because of the work God had done in Paul's life, he was able to minister to others. Paul, a good steward of this enabling power, greatly influenced others through his preaching, teaching, and writing. He compared himself to a wise builder. He at times built only the foundation, but because he fashioned it according to the grace of God, another could continue to build. Paul admitted that his labors were successful only because the grace of God worked through him: "But by the grace of God I am what I am: and his grace which was bestowed upon me was not in vain; but I laboured more abundantly than they all: yet not I, but the grace of God which was with me"(1 Corinthians 15:10).

Since we cannot give to others what we don't have, we need to look to Him for strength and courage. In our quiet times with the Lord, He renews our strength. This time of refreshing should not be aimless wandering but an occasion to see His face, His strength, and His grace more clearly. When we submit to God's Word and surrender to His working in our lives, we can effectively minister to others with the truths that God has taught us. We can demonstrate God's power to change and mold us as He desires through our transparent efforts. We point others to Him.

With any service come trials and disappointments. God's grace will comfort and restore our weary-in-well-doing hearts when we stop ministering to others in our strength and rest in His grace! Our own strength will fail, but His grace, His enabling power, will energize us to serve others daily. We must settle for nothing less. Those around us need to see His strength, not our weakness; His love, not our fear; and His grace, not our emptiness. He must be lifted up!

Grace is necessary . . .
- for strength to endure.
- for wisdom to be effective.
- for courage to stand the tests.
- for love to love the unlovely.
- for healing to mend the wounds.

We are weak, unworthy, and inadequate for the tasks we face as we serve others. But when we are willing to face our inabilities, we are then ready to claim God's grace that will match our weaknesses, unworthiness, and inadequacies. It is by appropriating this grace that effective ministry can begin. We must serve others with the power of another—our Lord Jesus!

He Gives Grace to Wait Patiently

Even with the routine activities of any given day, I often want to know what lies ahead. When times of important decisions and life-changing questions arise, I struggle to wait on God for the unfolding of His will. Yet if I am resting in His grace, I will wait patiently for God to show me His plan. If I am trusting God, I will believe that His grace is sufficient to enable me to wait. "My son, give me thine heart, and let thine eyes observe my ways" (Proverbs 23:2).

God asks us to give our focused attention to Him and then sit back and watch Him work. Then when He shows us what we are to do, we should obey His leading. We often complicate His clear guidance with our lack of faith. He declares two easy steps for us: "Give Me thine heart" and "Watch Me work!"

When you find yourself weak and weary, are you trusting in your own strength and abilities instead of resting in the grace of God? Our trials, ministries, and decisions will overwhelm us when we deal with them in our wisdom. Give your heart to the Lord in full surrender, rest in His marvelous grace, and watch Him work! "Now our Lord Jesus Christ himself, and God, even our Father, which hath loved us, and hath given us everlasting consolation and good hope through grace, comfort your hearts, and stablish you in every good word and work" (2 Thessalonians 2:16–17).

My Heart Restored

My heart was grieved as my church family shared their endless prayer requests during a Wednesday night service. The events of the past year played a part in the burden we all felt. Many in our church family had faced the death of loved ones—husbands, wives, mothers, and daughters—so many in one year.

Our hearts were heavy as our pastor shared the potentially serious medical condition just discovered in their two-month-old son. The possible diagnosis seemed too drastic for any of us to comprehend; yet, the doctor had spoken with guarded confidence at best. The next day this little guy would undergo further tests to confirm or deny the first prognosis. Our pastor shared the confidence in God and His grace that they were claiming. What a long night it must have been for them as they waited the further testing that the morning would bring.

But the evening didn't end there. As I prayed with a dear elderly lady, she introduced me to the daughter-in-law of a friend—a friend I had lost touch with over the past eight years. Before our prayer time

God's

grace

is

sufficient

and

abundant

was over, I learned that her mother-in-law, my friend, was waiting for the answer to the health issues she was facing. The conditions being explored were rare and incurable. I pray almost daily for this ministry-wife friend. My heart ached as I realized that I had been totally unaware of what she was facing, yet God had kept her on my heart and in my prayers for many years. Our lives touched only a few times. She had graciously accepted me at a time when I felt alone; her friendship probably had meant more to me than she had realized. I asked the daughter-in-law to give this friend my love and promise for continued prayers, but I wondered if she would remember.

I rejoice to see God's grace openly manifested in scores of lives and situations. At times when our world seems to be crumbling, are we claiming God's grace, God's power, to keep going? His grace has been promised to us in the necessary proportions—great grace for great needs, sudden grace for sudden needs, dying grace for dying, and comforting grace for those left behind. Do I doubt that God's grace is abundant enough for all these situations at one time? My head says to doubt. My heart claims His grace.

He alone is the comfort these dear people need. Our encouragement and love may help ease their load, but only the Lord can grant them the grace to walk through such difficult days. God's grace is sufficient and abundant. His grace matches our every need. May our weary souls rest and serve through His indescribable grace!

Restored Through His Forgiveness

Life offers unending choices. Some choices come naturally for us because of our personalities or circumstances. Other decisions are not so easy to make. We struggle to know which option is best. One such difficult choice is forgiveness. Too often we think of forgiveness as a natural outpouring of a loving heart responding to the penitent pleas of the offender. This is rarely the scenario.

Our reflexes quickly retract our hand from the painful heat of a flame; but our prideful heart refuses to recoil from the pain that accompanies the unforgiving heart. We feel that to forgive would be disrespectful of the pain we are savoring. Forgiveness comes when we willfully set aside both our pride and the offense.

Only a gracious, loving God could forgive our sins. He in His mercy does not give us what we deserve—righteous judgment. Instead, He offers forgiveness through the death and resurrection of

Jesus. When we believe and receive the Lord Jesus as our Savior, our sins are forgiven.

We struggle with defeat when we live with unconfessed sin and an unforgiving heart. We can know His continuing forgiveness while we walk through life as His child. And by His grace, we can learn to forgive others by following His example. Restoration can be ours when we claim God's forgiveness. "And be ye kind one to another, tenderhearted, forgiving one another, even as God for Christ's sake hath forgiven you" (Ephesians 4:32).

He restores my fellowship with Him when my sin is confessed and forgiven and when I forgive others.

He Restores My Fellowship

If we find ourselves discouraged, we need to look closer at our fellowship with the Lord. Many times that fellowship is broken because of sin in our lives. How often do we let bitterness, anger, jealousy, disobedience, gossip, or laziness go unchecked because we believe them to be an acceptable reply to the trials of life? However, God's Word does not give us such exemptions. Suffering in this life doesn't justify sin. Sin grieves God and breaks fellowship with Him—a fellowship that is essential to walk in victory.

Instead of ignoring our sinful attitudes and behaviors, we need to set aside all the excuses, identify the sin, and confess it. Sin breaks our fellowship with God, and that broken fellowship leaves us with a burden of guilt that depletes our joy and peace. Our salvation is still secure in the work of the Lord Jesus, but the vital communion that we need with God is hindered. It is a joy to know that He eagerly awaits the opportunity to forgive us. When we confess our sin to Him, He promises not only to forgive but to do so abundantly. Isaiah says, "Let the wicked forsake his way, and the unrighteous man his thoughts:

and let him return unto the Lord, and he will have mercy upon him; and to our God, for he will abundantly pardon" (55:7).

God has mercy on those who come to Him when they confess their sinful actions and thoughts. God's pardon is unlimited; it is abundant. *Abundantly* is defined as "in plentiful supply; more than sufficient, ample; abounding with; rich."[1] God is ready and waiting. We may have to labor to forgive others, but God readily forgives us. His mercy is plenteous; His pardon is complete. With forgiveness comes a renewed relationship like a child being forgiven by a loving parent. God's forgiveness is declared throughout Scripture.

- God is ready to forgive my sin. His mercy is plenteous to all who call on Him (Psalm 86:5).
- God chooses to not remember my sin (Jeremiah 31:34).
- God provides redemption and forgiveness of our sins through the shed blood of the Lord Jesus—not because of anything we have done (Colossians 1:13–14).

The Pictures of Forgiveness

One of my sons-in-law is an attorney. When he finished law school, he was not allowed to practice law immediately. He was first required to take the bar exam to see if he truly understood the law that he had diligently studied. But just taking the exam did not give him the credentials to be a lawyer. He had to wait for several months to learn if his score on the test was sufficient proof of what he had learned. When the scores were finally posted, he then had to wait until he was officially sworn in by the state of South Carolina. Anything that he might have tried to do before that ceremony would not have been binding or legal; he was not officially an attorney until the state declared him to be.

God is our righteous, holy judge. All He does is legal and binding. All His Word is legal and binding. He does not need the approval of anyone. When He declares our standing before Him, it is without question. We are forgiven because of the work of Christ on the cross! The scope and magnitude of our sin can be staggering when we see the perfection of God. At times, we may feel uncertain that a holy God could possibly want to forgive us. God illustrates His forgiveness in several ways to help us picture, and therefore understand, His gracious forgiveness.

As Far as the East Is from the West

The psalmist says, "He hath not dealt with us after our sins; nor rewarded us according to our iniquities. . . . As far as the east is from the west, so far hath he removed our transgressions from us" (103:10, 12). God deals with our sin based on His mercy and grace and removes our sins as far as the east is from the west. God's forgiveness cannot be illustrated with the directions of north and south. North eventually changes to south and the picture of sin's removal would be lost. God's forgiveness is total, complete, and unconditional.

Behind His Back

Isaiah declared, "Behold, for peace I had great bitterness: but thou hast in love to my soul delivered it from the pit of corruption: for thou hast cast all my sins behind thy back" (38:17). God puts our sins behind His back completely out of His sight. God deals with our sin in loving-kindness. He delivers us from the corruption of our sin. He molds us into the image of His Son.

Blotted Out

God says of Himself that "I, even I, am he that blotteth out thy transgressions for mine own sake, and will not remember thy sins" (Isaiah 43:25). Through this legal act, He blots out our sins and chooses to not remember them. His forgiveness is complete and absolute. He will never recall these confessed and forgiven sins.

Depths of the Sea

Micah 7:19 says that God "will turn again, he will have compassion upon us; he will subdue our iniquities; and thou wilt cast all their sins into the depths of the sea." Because of God's great compassion, He casts our confessed sins into the depths of the sea. The ocean's deepest spot known to man is the Marianas Trench. Measuring almost seven miles deep, it is located in the western North Pacific Ocean near Guam. Our sins can never be recovered and held against us.

An IOU

Paul states, "Blotting out the handwriting of ordinances that was against us, which was contrary to us, and took it out of the way, nailing it to his cross" (Colossians 2:14). Our sins are pictured as a long list that has been nailed to Christ's cross. This list is like a signed IOU that has been blotted out or covered up with ink. The sins are now unreadable—forgiven.

The Blessings of Forgiveness

Do you remember the fun of a friendly game of hide and seek? Whether we were playing it as children or later in life with children, it was a great time! Remember the hiding places a small child chooses? His creative spot might not fully conceal him, but he squeals with joy when the adult pretends not to find him. The game can last for hours as the turns for hiding and counting are exchanged.

David's hiding place here in Psalm 32 had a far more serious context. He said, "Blessed is he whose transgression is forgiven, whose sin is covered. . . . Thou art my hiding place; thou shalt preserve me from trouble; thou shalt compass me about with songs of deliverance" (Psalm 32:1, 7). David often needed a place to safely hide from his enemies. He knew the joy of resting securely in the arms of his Lord. That rest could come only after sins were confessed and forsaken.

In this psalm, David declared the blessings of being forgiven (verses 1–2). Unconfessed sin devastated David (verses 3–4), but confessing those sins to God brought forgiveness and joy (verses 5, 11). With his sins forgiven, David experienced the communion of prayer, the security of instruction, and the peace of trusting (verses 6, 8, 10).

What sins do you need to confess to the Lord? Remember that He has promised to be faithful to forgive our sins when we bring them to Him: "If we confess our sins, he is faithful and just to forgive us our sins, and to cleanse us from all unrighteousness" (1 John 1:9). Don't miss the joy and fellowship with God that can be yours! He longs to be your hiding place.

HE REMOVES THE WEIGHT OF GUILT

His promises are true. We must first call our sin what God calls it. Too many times we try to justify our thoughts and actions instead of dealing with them honestly before God. When we are willing to affirm our sin, God promises to forgive. The guilt of sin can weigh heavy on our heart even after we confess it. Satan often bombards us with doubts about our sincerity and about God's ability to forgive. When we consider our part and God's part in forgiveness, we soon realize that He does all the work of forgiveness.

- My Part: I must confess my sin, or call my sin what God calls it.

- God's Part: He is faithful and just to forgive our sins.

- My Part: I must believe in Him.

- God's Part: God gives me the forgiveness of my sins.

- My Part: I must confess my sin to God in prayer.

- God's Part: God will hear my prayers and forgive.

When we understand God's desire to forgive, we also need to realize that Satan endeavors to make us believe we should not forgive ourselves. Someone might say, "But you don't know what I've done! God maybe has forgiven me, but I can't forgive myself." To refuse this personal forgiveness means we doubt

- the grace of God—His favor to the undeserving.
- the power of God—His ability to forgive our sins.
- the Word of God—its declaration of the status of our sin in His sight.
- the power of Christ's blood—its sufficiency to atone for our sin.

Satan uses these doubts to keep us defeated. We cannot have victory over sin in our lives if we continually struggle with God's gracious forgiveness. If we could deserve or earn this pardon, it would not be by grace. Nowhere in Scripture do we see any limits to God's ability to forgive when we confess our sin to Him. To acknowledge our sin before God is a humbling thing, but there is victory through the Lord Jesus! Forgiveness is a gift of grace.

If we cannot forgive ourselves, we may not fully understand the richness of Christ's work on the cross. Our standing in Jesus Christ was provided by His death. In Romans 4:7 we learn that we can rejoice in our forgiveness; our sins are forgiven, covered up, and no longer visible to a holy God. The Lord Jesus is able to forgive completely because the forgiveness is based on the riches of His grace, not our merit (Ephesians 1:7). We find forgiveness not because of who we are but because of Who the Lord Jesus is. We will one day be presented to God as blameless in His sight—free of all charges. God will see us as perfectly holy because He will see us through the shed blood of Jesus. We then must strive to see ourselves as God sees us—sinners whose sins are covered and paid for by the precious blood of the Lord Jesus Christ. Every time you are tempted to question your forgiveness, praise God instead! He has forgiven you!

◉⟫⟫⟫ ◉⟩ HE RENEWS MY PASSION TO LOVE HIM MORE ⟨◉ ⟨⟨⟨⟨◉

I once declared my new motto to be "I will not be disappointed when people disappoint me." The Lord was teaching me through various struggles that only He would never let me down. Man would; He could not. Yet, here I was again facing the unbelievable—a friend's deception.

As I prepared a Bible study lesson from Ephesians 4, I found a phrase that challenged my disappointed heart—"longsuffering, forbearing one another in love." I began to study that phrase with new desire. The deeper I went into the meaning of the words, the greater my heart was challenged. I concluded that God was asking me not only to be patient with the one who had caused my hurt but also to tolerate in a spirit of love whatever another person did.

The forbearance of God is a truth so closely related to forgiveness that the one should not be considered without the other. Forbearance is the suffering of negative circumstances without giving in to them. Forbearance involves patiently tolerating wrongs or difficulties. It means "to endure, tolerate."[2] Forbearance is the outgrowth of humility and gentleness—a "gracious way of putting up with the faults of others."[3] Forbearance puts up with difficulties while continuing to love the one who caused the problem. The thought of such an attitude is overwhelming and insurmountable until we realize that God is not asking us to accomplish this in our strength. He has set the example, and He will supply the grace, the power, to bring this about in our life.

When I realize how often I must disappoint my Lord, I stand in awe of His amazing love and grace. In His forbearance, He is patient with me! God's unconditional, unchanging love for me is magnificently pictured in His forbearance. In spite of our best efforts, we fall short of what He desires us to be. We make choices, decisions, and plans that He finds disappointing and displeasing to Him. Because God lovingly waits for me to come to Him for forgiveness, my heart should be drawn to Him with greater love and devotion. He waited for me to realize my need of a Savior. He continues to wait for me to confess my sin and ask His forgiveness. And His love never wavers. How can my love for Him not grow deeper!

Although God's forbearance is continually seen, His wrath cannot be suspended indefinitely if the sinner does not accept God's conditions. Forbearance is also God's withholding punishment, giving man time to come to Him for salvation and forgiveness.

However, we must never presume on the forbearance of God. He is also holy and just. Second Corinthians 6:2 states, "Behold, now is the accepted time; behold, now is the day of salvation."

He Renews My Compassion for Others

While we minister to those around us, we can become weary and discouraged if they don't readily respond to the truths of God's Word. With His help, we must remember His patient and loving heart toward those for whom He waits. We must faithfully present the Lord to others, but only He can draw them to Himself. He waits, and so must we, for people to receive the message of His Word. This patience is a fruit of the Spirit that He desires to grow in our life. Since He daily demonstrates forbearance to us, how can we not show it toward those around us? God sets the example and then equips us to pursue His likeness. Our weary heart is refreshed when we understand His loving patience, and our passion should be renewed to faithfully love and minister to others for His glory.

There are many biblical examples of forgiveness and forbearance. Noah gives us a beautiful picture of God's forbearance and also Noah's as he prepared for the destruction of the earth by a worldwide flood: "By faith Noah, being warned of God of things not seen as yet, moved with fear, prepared an ark to the saving of his house; by the which he condemned the world, and became heir of the righteousness which is by faith" (Hebrews 11:7).

God's forbearance was evident as He gave the people of Noah's day 120 years to turn from their wickedness. God could have destroyed the earth without warning; but God directed Noah to build the ark knowing it would be many years before the project could be completed. God protected Noah and his family as they built the ark and preached repentance to the world.

Noah displayed forbearance as well. With no comprehension of rain, Noah obeyed God; he had no doubt that God could be trusted. In spite of ridicule and opposition, Noah devotedly preached to his neighbors and friends a strong warning of coming judgment. Noah remained true to God and courageously stood alone. Genuinely trusting God, Noah became an heir of righteousness by faith. As long and discouraging as those years must have been, God blessed Noah and his family for their forbearance—their patient endurance through the years of preaching and building.

My Heart Restored

Endless emotions from the past and present swirled around me as we attended the funeral of the man who had disappointed me in spite of my resolve. Only a few gathered to pay their respects and remember his life. What a blessing it was to know that he had the assurance of his salvation. The past ten months had given ample time for him to show that he was confident in his salvation.

I remember the Saturday night years ago when he called to accept my husband's offer to join us for church the next morning. When David went to work for him, he had invited him several times to join us. He had declined the invitation until this night. We saved him a seat and knew at the end of the service that he would be back but not alone—his family would be with him.

Over the next few years, we had the joy of seeing his wife saved, a woman from the office and her mother saved, and many others come to church with us to hear the gospel proclaimed. There were Sundays when an entire row was filled with co-workers. When the office closed and some problems were fully disclosed, our hearts were broken and our friends were scattered. But through the months that followed, our hearts grew in biblical forbearance and forgiveness. By the time this family returned to our city and church, through God's grace, we welcomed them home.

My heart ached as I said goodbye to this dear young widow and her three small children. What lies ahead for them, I have no idea. But I know that God holds their future and by His loving grace He will see them through the difficult days ahead.

I thank the Lord for allowing us the opportunity to forgive this man and demonstrate that forgiveness to him over the past months. I praise God for challenging me to forgive and love someone who had hurt my family. As I stood by his casket, I had no regrets. I'd forgiven him many months ago. Only God can give us the forbearance and love to forgive; in our flesh, it is impossible. Because of God's continual faithfulness, we can know and live a life of victory. Who in your life should you forgive? What sins are you excusing and not confessing and forsaking? May your weary heart be restored as you know the joy of His eternal forgiveness!

Only God can give us the forbearance and love to forgive

Remade in His Likeness

CHAPTER NINE

My heart was warmed by precious memories when I saw the title of the song we were about to sing. My father had introduced this wonderful chorus to me when I was a little girl. To many this father-daughter lesson might not seem unique or exceptional; but in my case, it was. My mother taught me scores of songs through my early years. Her many children's ministries always included old hymns as well as new songs based on biblical truths. My mother gave me a love for music and a desire to use it to minister to others. Although my dad loved music and encouraged my sisters and me to develop our talents, his abilities in the field of music were limited to appreciation only.

While away preaching one weekend, my father came home with the words and melody of a new song firmly fixed in his mind. He had my oldest sister follow his rendition of the melody until his ear told him it was accurate. I have no idea how long it took for them to sort through the pitches. When the words were added, I realized, even as a little girl, that the words were what had endeared my father to this new song.

> His name is Wonderful,
> His name is Wonderful,
> His name is Wonderful,
> Jesus my Lord;
> He is the mighty King,
> Master of everything,
> His name is Wonderful,
> Jesus my Lord.
>
> He's the great Shepherd,
> the Rock of all ages,
> Almighty God is He;
> Bow down before Him,
> Love and adore Him,
> His name is Wonderful,
> Jesus my Lord.

Audrey Mieir[1]

Later we found the music to this song we had grown to love. Amazingly my father's version was very accurate. This dear chorus has remained one of my favorites all through the years. The names of God have given me comfort and encouragement on a daily basis, and this precious song often flows from my heart as I meditate on Who He is. I'm thankful for that day many years ago when my father brought this precious song home with him!

We need restoring when we lose sight of the Lord Jesus, the One so beautifully characterized in this little song. We become frustrated when we try to live the Christian life in our own abilities and strengths, instead of focusing on Jesus. With our eyes fixed on the

Savior, He can mold us into His image. We should anticipate the day
that we will "be like him; for we shall see him as he is" (1 John 3:2).

He remakes me into His likeness through a daily process called sanctification.

Sanctification involves a continuous conforming of my life to
His image. This process will be complete when I go to heaven to be
with Him and am immediately transformed into His likeness.

God begins a good work in us the moment we trust Christ as
Savior. Immediately "old things are passed away; behold, all things
are become new" (2 Corinthians 5:17). The theological term for this
change is *sanctification*. Sanctification can be defined as "the radical
change God brings about in the heart of a person who trusts Christ
as Savior."[2] This marvelous work is done in us—not by us. From
this moment, God sees us as righteous because He sees us through
the blood of the Lord Jesus.

God continues this process of conforming us to the image of
the Lord Jesus by the power of the gospel throughout our life. This
transformation will be complete when we step into the presence of
the Lord. Our goal in this life should be to daily set our focus on the
Lord to better reflect His glory. When others look at us, they should
see our Savior! Paul says, "I beseech you therefore, brethren, by the
mercies of God, that ye present your bodies a living sacrifice, holy,
acceptable unto God, which is your reasonable service. And be not
conformed to this world: but be ye transformed by the renewing of
your mind, that ye may prove what is that good, and acceptable, and
perfect, will of God" (Romans 12:1–2).

"But we all, with open face beholding as in a glass the glory of
the Lord, are changed into the same image from glory to glory, even
as by the Spirit of the Lord" (2 Corinthians 3:18). Sanctification requires surrender and surrender demands obedience. To simply hear
or read God's Word is not enough. We must demonstrate His Word

through our obedient actions. God gives us what we need to obey His truths, and through our obedience He changes us. Until we enter our eternal home in heaven, He gives us the desire, the power, and the ability to be a reflection of His likeness.

His Example

God gives us a clear example to follow. Throughout the pages of the Old Testament, we are introduced to the character of God as He deals with man. His holiness, His character, His sovereignty, His wisdom and much more are plainly declared. Many times we are commanded to be holy as He is holy. In the New Testament, we follow the life of the Lord Jesus as He, God the Son, ministered to mankind and then gave His life on the cross. Through His life, death, and resurrection, the faithful reader learns the pattern to copy.

In this life, we continually face the temptation and ability to sin. We must set aside what comes naturally to our sinful hearts and by His grace adopt the characteristics and actions of our Lord. Many verses explain what we must "put off" and what we must "put on" to be Christlike. Remember that we cannot make these changes in our strength. Through the grace of God, we are able to surrender to Him, separate from sin, and mirror the character of Christ.

Galatians 5:19–24, Ephesians 4:22–32, and Colossians 3:5–17 clearly describe what changes we should be striving for. Carefully consider these lists to see what to put off that God despises and what to put on to bear His likeness.

Put Off

Put off adultery, idolatry, hatred, strife, anger, divisiveness, murder, drunkenness, pride, envy, jealousy, lust, covetousness, selfish ambition, the flesh and its desires, your former lifestyle, deceitful lusts, lying, wrath, sin, the Devil's control, stealing, corrupt words, bitterness, wrath, anger, evil speaking, malice, clamor, quarreling, immorality, jealousy, blasphemy, and filthy words.

PUT ON

Put on love, joy peace, patience, goodness, faithfulness, self-control, a renewed spirit of your mind, the new man created in righteousness and true holiness, good works, giving to the needy, edifying words, kindness, forgiveness, compassion, humility, gentleness, forbearance, thankfulness, and actions that glorify God.

Being a grandmother is a great joy! The position had been highly recommended, but now that I'm the grandma of two precious little girls, it's even better than anyone could describe. Since they were just a few months old, both girls love to see themselves in a mirror. Whether a mirror on a toy or one on a wall, their little faces light up when they see the baby looking back at them. Even when life seems a bit sad, their smiles appear with the glimpse of the other baby.

Who do others see when they look at you? Do they see your face reflecting your sinful heart? Or do they see the reflection of your gracious Savior? Is your focus on Him unwavering? Regardless of your circumstances, do you mirror His goodness?

HIS MIND

We can know the mind of God as we read and study His Word. He reveals to us His thoughts and commands us to "let this mind be in [us] which was also in Christ Jesus" (Philippians 2:5). Our sinful mind must be transformed to become like the mind of Jesus. This transformation comes only in the study of and surrender to the Word of God. To know His mind, we must know Him. To know Him, we must know His Word! Deuteronomy 10:12 says, "What doth the Lord thy God require of thee, but to fear the Lord thy God, to walk in all his ways, and to love him and to serve the Lord thy God with all thy heart and with all thy soul?"

We realize that God's thoughts and ways are far beyond our comprehension. The Lord declares through the prophet Isaiah, "For my thoughts are not your thoughts, neither are your ways my ways. . . . For as the heavens are higher than the earth, so are my ways higher than your ways, and my thoughts than your thoughts" (Isaiah 55:8–9). He enables us to glimpse His splendor when we read, study, and obey His Word. "God's sovereignty and omniscience are extolled by the statement that His thoughts (i.e., purposes or intentions) and ways (. . . 'directions') are higher than ours. While God may certainly be known by men, He is still incomprehensible in the totality of His person and purposes. Therefore, He reveals Himself to men by His word."[3]

Oh, the truths that have been taught through the use of flannel graph! With all the latest in graphic art, I'm not sure this form of illustration from my childhood is still used or available. But as a little girl, the colorful way to illustrate Bible stories and Bible truths was on a flannelgraph board with these vibrant pictures. How our imaginations re-created the biblical accounts!

Our children's church lessons were centered on Bible people who had to decide if they were going to follow God or their own desires. When the conflict had been presented, the teacher would change the flannel graph from the biblical scene to a simple house-shaped piece with two men inside. The house represented the person and the two men pictured the struggle between the spirit and the flesh. "Newman," young, strong, and handsome, represented the spiritual life we receive at salvation. "Rufus," older and gruff-appearing, illustrated the flesh that desires to rule even after salvation.

Whatever the conflict in the story, the two men illustrated the struggle that went on within the heart of the Bible character. If the person desired to obey God and was walking with God, Newman would be stronger and victorious. If the person stubbornly resisted what was right and yielded to sinful desires, Rufus would overtake Newman. The teacher put it in simple terms—whichever man was fed the most would be stronger and therefore victorious.

However trite this battle may seem in our twenty-first-century way of thinking, this picture has come to my mind throughout the years when I faced difficult situations. My heart is reminded to feed my spirit and, with God's strength, conquer my flesh. If I turn my longings to the things of this world, I'll lose the battle! Though I desire to follow the Lord's example, I can succumb to the powerful influence of my ever-present flesh if my focus on Christ is distracted. Who are you "feeding?" Is your thinking obediently submitted to Christ? Or are you trying to live your Christian life while still nurturing your flesh?

> **He is remaking me into His likeness through a plan**
> **designed uniquely for me that concludes with me**
> **being with Him in heaven "as he is" (1 John 3:2).**

To think of reflecting the image of our Savior may overwhelm rather than refresh us. The reality of our sin can become so great that any attempt at Christlikeness can quickly be abandoned as hopeless. The grace of God is vital to this process. It is the plan of God that by His grace every believer manifests the glorious image of His Son throughout this life. This agenda is not reserved for the religious elite or scholarly but for all who receive His gracious gift of salvation. All the events of life, even the seasons of weariness, are avenues for the grace of God to transform our lives. His plan also includes the glorious fulfillment when we are finally in His heavenly presence. We will be with Him and we will be like Him because we shall see Him face to face! John says, "Beloved, now are we the sons of God, and it doth not yet appear what we shall be: but we know that, when he shall appear, we shall be like him; for we shall see him as he is" (1 John 3:2).

The following verses describe God's plan for a believer's life, which includes a resurrected body like that of the Lord Jesus. The inspired writers of Scripture used a variety of images to portray this process for us.

- Our destiny is to be made into His image—the *firstborn* of many more to follow (Romans 8:29).
- We are like a *seed* being planted and then bringing forth life (1 Corinthians 15:36–38).
- The birth of a *baby*, the bringing forth of new life and the labor involved, demonstrates Christ forming a new life in us (Galatians 4:19).
- We are like a *runner* running a race with our focus on the finish line. We press on to reach this high calling (Philippians 3:12–14).
- We are called the *sons of God*. When He shall appear, we will be like Him because we will see Him exactly as He is (1 John 3:2).

His Workmanship

Growing more like our Lord is an on-going process through the course of our lives. We are His workmanship, His creation, which is taken from sinful materials at salvation and changed into the extraordinary work of the master craftsman. The prophet Isaiah likened God's work to that of a potter and his clay.

We have a longtime friend who is an extremely talented artist. He creates incredible beauty in various art forms. One of the most fascinating things I've seen him do is to throw a pot on a potter's wheel. The clay is under his control. When it is placed on the wheel, it has no form or shape of its own. The useless, lifeless form serves no purpose. It is only through the pressure and skill of his hands and the motion of the wheel that this material takes on shape and therefore purpose. The clay has no voice in what it is to become. He determines what is best and is relentless in shaping the clay to his desired design.

My friend's wisdom is reflected in the finished vessel. With careful eye, he studies the clay as it takes form on the wheel. If the slightest imperfection surfaces, he stops this delicate process, crushes the clay, and begins the reshaping. A marred vessel would not function in the way he intended and would bring reproach to his reputation. If an imperfection remains hidden until after the vessel is finished, the vessel will be broken. Its function must not be flawed.

Both Isaiah and Jeremiah compared Israel to a lump of clay many times. The common vessels and familiar skill vividly depicted Israel in the hand of God. But the comparison isn't limited to Israel. We, too, are like the clay in the hand of God. The wheel comes in various forms and venues in our lives, but God uses each one with a variety of pressures to mold us into His image. May we be as submissive to the hand of God as the clay is to the hand of the potter. For us to function according to His purpose, God must at times reshape us to correct our sinful hearts. May we not resist His sovereign working even if it is painful. We should simply surrender to His loving touch, allowing Him to make us a trophy of His masterful hand.

His Servants

God may give us leaders whose examples we can follow. Paul challenged believers to walk as he did. We must never let the example of man take precedent over God Himself. Man's flesh is always present and even the godliest can give in to temptation and sin. We can follow man only as he or she follows God.

We are called to be a good example to those around us. People are watching us even when we are unaware of it. We should never encourage others to imitate us but always point others to our Savior and Lord. Help those around you keep their focus on God by living a life that points to Him: "In all things shewing thyself a pattern of good works: in doctrine shewing uncorruptness, gravity, sincerity, sound speech, that cannot be condemned; that he that is of the contrary part may be ashamed, having no evil thing to say of you. . . . These things speak, and exhort, and rebuke with all authority. Let no man despise thee" (Titus 2:7–8, 15).

According to these verses in Titus, our example should be worth following and above reproach. Our progress in this area should be an example that others can follow. Could you challenge those around you to follow you? Do you desire to become more Christlike or are you following the lifestyle of this world? Surrendering to His working in our lives is a vital step to being remade into His likeness.

We sometimes find ourselves struggling because we cannot fix what those we love are facing. We may be doing all we can—all they are asking us to do. But our help seems futile. We want to solve their dilemmas. But do these situations serve a purpose? Could it be that God is using these circumstances as the potter's wheel to bring these precious vessels, our loved ones, closer to Him? He works through the pain to bring us to the place of His comfort. We must learn to let God work and thank Him for the trials in others' lives as well as the ones in our lives.

- It is in our weakness that He becomes our strength.
- It is in our sorrows that He becomes our comfort.
- It is in our poverty that He becomes our wealth.
- It is in our uncertainty that He becomes our guide.
- It is in our fear that He becomes our consolation.
- It is in our discouragement that He becomes our joy.
- It is in our loneliness that He becomes our dearest friend.

We must not be anxious. Everything is within the plan of a wise and loving God. He is at work. He is the master designer of all the details of our lives. May we learn to welcome the trials of this life. It is through these obstacles that God shows Himself most clearly. May the Lord use us in the lives of those we love. May we point them to the Savior. May we encourage them, pray for them, and love them. May we be ministers of grace to help them become more like Christ.

My Heart Restored

My dad loved to build things. I remember the desk, beds, cupboard, and other wooden furniture that my dad made for my sisters and me. I was my dad's apprentice. Watching him build, I would hand him tools and ask him questions by the hours. I'm sure my finding him tools was to give his weary ears a rest—not just to obtain my assistance. I thought he could fabricate anything. All he needed was the right materials and my admiring gaze.

Sometimes he worked on things that were designated for a Christmas or birthday gift. Those were projects that I could not share. Trying desperately to confirm what my vivid imagination was picturing, I would longingly perch at the top of the basement stairs to talk to him. My curiosity would all but overtake me as I waited for the morning that he would bestow the gift.

When he finished the item, it was always far more wonderful than I could have imagined. Why? My father had made it for me. I had seen it being fashioned piece-by-piece—sometimes by my father's side and sometimes only in my imagination. Because my father had made it, it was wonderful!

So it is with my heavenly Father. I don't always see and comprehend what He is doing. Many times I stand in curious confusion trying to catch a glimpse of His intent. Other times I see the pieces coming together, yet still I am not able to imagine what the final outcome will resemble. But I'm learning, far too slowly, that God is in control of this project called my life. The events that are shaping my days are ordered and fashioned by His all-powerful, all-knowing hand. May we trust our Lord without reservation. He, the master carpenter, is remaking us into His likeness!

God is in control of this project called my life

Reaching Out to Others

CHAPTER TEN

As fall approached to end my rocking-chair summer, my weary heart was mending. But there was still an essential piece missing; I could not know the complete joy of a heart restored until I began to reach out to others. I had become so focused on my own struggle that I had set aside the needs of others. I was still caring for my family and ministering to the women in my church, but I lacked the genuine compassion of my Savior. It was time for me to start sharing the unconditional and gracious love of the Lord Jesus. That summer at the feet of the Master had changed my view of friendship. I didn't need a friend. I needed to be a friend.

Instead of returning to teach in our Christian school that fall, I took a position as an assistant in a medical office of fourteen doctors. The staff to provide the care for these scores of patients was numerous. My duties were simple, but through them I slowly began to serve with a new resolve. I had a new mission field—to a few who were saved and to most who were not. My weary heart continued to heal as I befriended my new co-workers and attempted to apply the truths I'd learned during my time alone with God.

God desires us to lovingly serve all who are around us. Encouragement and friendship between Christians are also crucial. The idea of fellowship may seem too mundane in the depths of our weariness. The lack of godly friends may make having someone to rejoice with seem impossible. Often women share with me the problems they have encountered with other believers. It is painful to experience hurtful words or unkind actions from those we wish were encouraging us. Satan takes great pleasure in causing divisions among God's people. Knowing this conflict would be common, Jesus clearly taught His disciples that their testimonies to the world would be based on their love for each other: "By this shall all men know that ye are my disciples, if ye have love one to another" (John 13:35).

We need to love other Christians even when they are difficult to love. Nowhere in God's Word are we given license to love only the lovely. Would lost people around you know that you are a Christian by how you treat other Christians? Satan uses this conflict to limit the effectiveness of the message we proclaim. Our hearts may need restoring because we possess an unloving attitude toward other Christians or a cold indifference to the unsaved.

He restores me as I befriend those around me
whether they know the Lord as Savior or not.

He Restores Me Through
Fellowship with Other Christians

In 1 John, we are given specific guidelines of how to love other Christians. We need the friendship of Christians to stay encouraged in this sin-filled world. Let's look carefully at some key verses from this epistle and see what they teach on this important subject. John says, "That which we have seen and heard declare we unto you, that ye also may have fellowship with us: and truly our fellowship is with the Father, and with his Son Jesus Christ. . . . But if we walk in the light as he is in the light, we have fellowship one with another, and the blood of Jesus Christ his Son cleanseth us from all sin" (1 John 1:3, 7).

Our relationship with God determines our ability to fellowship with other Christians. Fellowship can be defined as "'a close association or relationship'; in Christian terms this means mutual acceptance of and submission to the verities of Christian faith. It means sharing in personal knowledge of and heartfelt obedience to God through Jesus Christ."[1] Fellowship with God and other Christians is possible only as we walk free from the bondage of sin.

Again, John says, "He that saith he is in the light, and hateth his brother, is in darkness even until now. He that loveth his brother abideth in the light, and there is none occasion of stumbling in him" (1 John 2:9–10). We cannot dislike our fellow Christians and be walking in obedience to the Lord. Although knowledge of biblical doctrines is of utmost importance, the accurate proclaiming of truth does not excuse a lack of godly compassion. This knowledge is worth little without love. Walking in a right relationship with the Lord will be evidenced in our relationships; we cannot have ungodly attitudes toward someone and be right with God.

God exemplified this message of love by giving the life of the Lord Jesus for us. We follow God's pattern of love when we serve others in unconditional, unselfish ways. Our love will be obvious through our deeds more than through our words. "Hereby perceive we the love of God, because he laid down his life for us: and we ought to lay down our lives for the brethren" (1 John 3:16). It's easy to say we love and care. But when we see a Christian with a need and do not help, we must ask ourselves, "Is God's love in me?" We cannot overlook the needs of others and claim to love them.

We often think that giving money is the only way to help others in need. Since few believe they have all the resources their lives require, they miss their obligation and opportunity to share. As Moses faced the burning bush in Exodus 4, he thought God's mission for him was impossible. What did he, a scared Israelite hiding in the wilderness, have that God could use to force Pharaoh to release the Hebrew people? God's answer to Moses was a simple question: "What is in your hand?"

When Moses responded to God's question, his life changed. God showed Moses that his shepherd's rod would give credence to God's demands. While Moses learned to do the miracles with the rod, God was preparing him for a great work to the Hebrew people. This rod was something common, simple, and available to Moses; no special task was required to obtain it. Moses simply had to use it as God directed!

What's in your hand that God can use to minister to those around you? God uses whatever we surrender to Him. Maybe it's food that you can share with a neighbor or church family. Maybe it's time that you spend writing a note or engaging in conversation. Watching a small child for the parent to run errands is a precious gift. When you look for the opportunities to help others, you'll be surprised what you will see to do. Reaching out to others in these gestures of love will refresh your soul and the weary heart of the recipient. Many uninterested hearts have responded to the gospel after having seen God's love demonstrated through the caring actions of a child of God.

"Beloved, if God so loved us, we ought also to love one another. . . . If a man say, I love God, and hateth his brother, he is a liar: for he that loveth not his brother whom he hath seen, how can he love God whom he hath not seen" (1 John 4:11, 20)? Is there bitterness and anger in your heart toward another Christian? That inner conflict will not be resolved without you facing your attitude, confessing your sin, and asking God's forgiveness. Until you go to that person and ask forgiveness, your fellowship with that person and with the Lord cannot be right! Whether the conflict involves a friend or family member, you must not ignore your responsibility in this area. Whom do you need to ask God to help you love? Remember, your love for the Lord is evidenced by your love for others.

⬣ ⟩⟩⟩ HE RESTORES ME WHEN I PRAISE HIM IN WORSHIP ⟨⟨⟨⬣

MY PRAISE

How much time do you spend praising God? To genuinely rejoice with others is difficult if we do not spend time praising God in private. Our refreshing will come as we thank God for all that He brings our way. Staying discouraged is impossible when we thank God for Who He is. We need to be known as grateful people who praise God. Seeing His loving hand in all that happens gives us hearts that can proclaim His greatness.

Sometimes our lives can be so demanding that we fail to see the opportunities to rejoice. Our burdens loom without apparent solutions. How can we praise God for what we desperately want removed? Once it is gone, maybe then we will be able to give God some positive feedback, but at the moment, positive is not possible.

Let's return to the account of Moses and ask again, "What is in your hand?" As God wanted to use Moses' rod for His glory, God wants to use what is in your hand for His glory too. Whether you are in a time of trial or on a mountaintop in revival, God wants you to give to Him what you are facing and let Him use it to bring Him glory. All that is happening to you is for God to build His holiness in you. His chastening, correction, and discipline are all for your best. They should bring you to a place of full surrender that is marked by a heart of praise.

When there seems to be no possible way of praising God for what we are experiencing, we can always praise Him for Who He is. Since He is unchanging, our praise can be unending. When we meditate on the attributes of God, we find it easy to rest and rejoice in God and in His arms of safety! This joy is contagious. When we rejoice in God, this delight will radiate from our hearts to those around us. Whether in private conversation or corporate worship, rejoicing refreshes the weary soul!

Have you taken the time to praise the Lord for the wonderful things He has done for you? In the busy, over-scheduled lives we live today, it is easy to let the days and weeks pass without thanking the Lord for all He is doing. The trials and burdens we face often consume our attention and overshadow the blessings. The psalmist was amazed at all God had done. His blessings were more than could be numbered!

Count Your Many Blessings

When upon life's billows you are tempest tossed,
When you are discouraged, thinking all is lost,
Count your many blessings, name them one by one,
And it will surprise you what the Lord has done.

Are you ever burdened with a load of care?
Does the cross seem heavy you are called to bear?
Count your many blessings, ev'ry doubt will fly,
And you will be singing as the days go by.

So, amid the conflict, whether great or small,
Do not be discouraged, God is over all;
Count your many blessings, angels will attend,
Help and comfort give you to your journey's end.

Count your blessings, name them one by one;

Count your blessings, see what God has done;

Count your blessings, name them one by one;

Count your many blessings, see what God has done.

Johnson Oatman Jr. [1]

Why not make a list of the "wonderful works" He has done in your life over the past few weeks? Spend time in prayer thanking and praising God for His many blessings! Share your blessings with another Christian.

My Worship

David in Psalm 34:3 says, "O magnify the Lord with me, and let us exalt his name together." Although private praise and worship are essential to walking with a heart of praise, we also need regular times of worship with other Christians. The writer of Hebrews says, "Not forsaking the assembling of ourselves together, as the manner of some is; but exhorting one another: and so much the more, as ye see the day approaching" (10:25). Our church services need to be times of refreshing as we set aside the routines of our lives and meet together. Wednesday evening prayer services often give me the encouragement I need to face the remainder of the week. During a service recently I left totally different from when I arrived. I started the service physically tired and overwhelmed, but the hymns we sang began the gradual transformation of my heart. "Like a River Glorious" especially spoke to my heart as I remembered "God's perfect peace." When praises and prayer requests were shared, my heart was lifted by the blessings experienced by others; the prayer needs put my life into perspective.

Next, our pastor reviewed the Sunday morning sermon about God ministering to Paul when he was overwhelmed. Our first prayer time was in complete silence—applying what God did for Paul in Acts 18 to our lives. A young man studying for the ministry preached from Psalm 40. He emphasized how David determined to be a testimony of righteousness and continual trust. And the final words of encouragement were from a friend I talked with as we walked to our cars after the service. Any one event would have ministered to my heart, but all these in one service! I left with new resolve and peace. What if I had chosen not to attend? What a blessing my weary heart would have missed!

Sometimes our attitudes can be addressed before we get to church. Many change into church faces on the drive to church without dealing with the issues of their heart. Do you try to use the hours before a service to prepare your heart? If you are harried, your heart is anything but prepared to focus on God's Word. Think about your normal Sunday morning. Are you helping the ones around you by having the right spirit in the services? Do you look forward to time at church or are you fulfilling some kind of expectation that you think others have for you? Or that you have for yourself? To truly find refreshing in fellowship with God's people, we must begin with our hearts prepared to receive with humility the truths from God's Word.

He Restores Me When I Share the Gospel

There is no greater way to restore our joy than to introduce someone to our Savior. We have a glorious gospel to share! When we keep our hearts tender to a lost and dying world, our responsibility stays a priority. If Satan can keep us looking at our weary hearts, we will miss seeing the lost souls around us. Our lives need to be in touch with those who have never heard the good news of salvation. Remember how Jesus boldly, but graciously, shared the gospel with those around Him while He was here on earth.

The Gospels are full of wonderful accounts of Jesus' ministry to the lost souls He encountered. At times, He preached to the multitudes about Who He was and their need of accepting Him as the

Messiah. At other times, He spoke with just one—quietly minister-ing to the individual's needs. One of my favorite biblical accounts is of Zaccheus meeting Jesus. Zaccheus devised a plan that would let him see Jesus of Nazareth. All the news about Jesus had captured his attention. Who was this man? Could it be Jesus Who held the secret to free his heart from its emptiness? As a tax collector, Zacch-eus was hated by the Jews for serving the Roman government and was scorned by the Romans for willingly extorting his own people.

Zaccheus longed for the chance to see Jesus. To talk to Him would be unlikely, but to see Him might be enough. Because of his stature, Zaccheus knew he would have to be creative to get a glimpse of Jesus. His best hope was to climb a sycamore tree beside the road Jesus was traveling. The view from the branch he chose was excellent. The Master might not see him, but Zaccheus knew he would be able to see Jesus.

Zaccheus's plan worked. As Jesus approached the tree, Zacch-eus was able both to see and hear Him. The closer Jesus came, the faster Zaccheus's heart beat. Could this truly be the Son of God? Although surrounded by the crowd, Jesus stopped, looked up, and turned His focus to Zaccheus. The acclaim of the multitude was exchanged for a dinner with a tax collector and his friends. Zacch-eus received Jesus as the Son of God and his Savior. He met Jesus on that road and Jesus changed him forever.

Jesus is never too busy to meet the needs of the individual, nor is He overwhelmed by the demands of the crowd. He willingly, lov-ingly gave His life for every individual in every crowd. We learn from Jesus' approach to the lost how we are to respond to the un-saved around us. We need to strive to share His gracious, genuine love for those who need to know Him. We need to emulate our Lord and daily extend the good news of the gospel to those whose lives we touch.

Take a few minutes to meditate on the following summary statements. Only God can make you graciously bold to the lost world around you.

- I must be around people who do not know my Savior.
- I must lovingly befriend and genuinely care for people around me.
- I must approach others with the gospel from their point of need.
- I must continually grow in the knowledge of God and His Word so that I can share the gospel with confidence.
- I must share the gospel with gracious boldness through the power of the Holy Spirit.

My Heart Restored

I had enjoyed the past few years of being a substitute teacher, but my husband and I decided that I needed to get a consistent part-time job. After dinner that Sunday, I opened the newspaper to check for part-time jobs. Normally that listing consists of the same couple ads for Avon and something mysteriously unnamed. But this day's entries included a spot just for me—dental instructor—and listed requirements that fit me perfectly. The one essential was a background in education. The astonishing detail was that I not only had the background in education but I also had over five years experience in the dental field. After faxing my resume, I was called for an interview and offered the position. I would be the dental educator for the local science center. The facilities and equipment were incredible, the hours were perfect, and the income was sufficient. I would be able to continue to write.

When I began my in-service training, I met my new co-workers. I was introduced to this new world that became my new mission field. I met many new people—people I'd have had no other opportunity to meet. Lives that I knew the Lord would have me befriend and love. And when my practice time was complete,

Discover

the joy and

healing

that comes

from serving

others with

the heart of

the Savior

I began working with children! Lots of children. Children on field trips. A room full of children twice a morning. Different children, teachers, and parents in every class. I have the opportunity, although brief, to touch their lives. My teaching topics may be dental related, but my heart's desire is to radiate God's love and grace. How amazing to realize that my few years of dental work coupled with my teaching led to such an opportunity. My rocking-chair summer had left me unsure if I would ever teach women or children again. As a dental assistant I was secluded from both. The Lord gave me back my teaching to women when my pastor asked me to teach the women's Bible study at my church, and now He'd given me the opportunity to again teach children.

Where are you? Whose life do you touch? May the Lord make us look beyond the faces and see the souls of those around us. May we see the lives that He wants us to touch with His grace. May He make His light shine through us so that all who enter our world will see Him in us. May our co-workers and friends recognize His love, compassion, and grace working in and through us. Oh, that we would allow the Lord to restore our weary souls and fulfill His divine purpose for us. May we reach out to others and discover the joy and healing that comes from serving others with the heart of the Savior.

Rejoicing in Hope

CHAPTER ELEVEN

To see a little child take his first steps is a memorable occasion. Many hours of practice precede the big moment. Over the course of many months, the child progresses through the developmental stages: rolling over, sitting up, crawling, pulling up, and walking with help. The skills he gradually learns finally lead to the first unassisted step! But along the way are setbacks—falls and tumbles—that leave the little one in tears but wiser. The number of times a child falls in the process of learning to walk must be amazing. No mother has the time to count such failures; but no mother forgets the look of accomplishment that floods the face of the little conqueror.

One thing, however, is certain: those falls are not wasted. Technique, balance, and determination are all growing with each failed attempt. It is only through the many ups and downs that everything comes to the correct balance and those first tiny, independent steps occur. Motivation is the overriding factor that brings the child success. Obtaining the desire overcomes all fear and frustration. The relentless pursuit to master the skill is rewarded with possession of the alluring goal.

> The steps of a good man are ordered by the Lord: and he delighteth in his way. Though he fall, he shall not be utterly cast down: for the Lord upholdeth him with his hand. (Psalm 37:23–24)

Did you ever think about how many lessons in life you learn through falling and needing restored? God orders our every step. He delights to see us diligently labor to become more like Him. He understands that many times we'll fall and fail, yet He continues to uphold us with His mighty hand. He never lets us go. His desires must be our goal. We must strive to be obedient to His Word. He knows that we will succeed only if we lean on Him. If the way were easy, we'd not need His strength to make it.

I wish I could tell you this restoration was only an isolated necessity—a process that once I passed through it I never needed to visit it again. But that is far from the case. As the years pass, I find my rocking chair to be a place I frequently visit. Some days I seem to enter a revolving door—leaving the weariness only briefly to make the circle right back to my chair. My life could be pictured as an upward spiral. I'm making progress in growing closer to my Lord, but I'm going in circles with the incline so gradual that my progress is realized only when I look backward. Daily I must refocus in at least one of these areas. My sinful heart is so slow to remember. The reality of the victory I experience today will be shadowed only by tomorrow's struggle.

It is God Who restores our weary souls. The times we need restoring are not without their purpose and benefit, for it is within this precious process that we learn the most. The more we practice these restorative steps, the quicker we find peace. When we recognize our need and seek our Savior, we come through the difficult time comprehending more of our sinfulness and more of our Savior's greatness.

>>>> >>>> >>>> >>>> WHAT WE LEARN <<<< <<<< <<<< <<<<

WE LEARN TO SEE GOD

In the midst of our struggle our sight can be so clouded that we can only look up—up to the Savior! The Savior Who loves us and intercedes on our behalf. Who wants us to quietly sit at His feet and worship Him alone. Who longs for us to trust Him with every detail of our lives. He requires no effort of us except our obedient surrender. Our time in God's Word and in prayer can reset our focus to begin this restorative process. We can discover perfect rest in God's amazing grace that saved us and now strengthens us.

WE LEARN TO SEE OURSELVES

We are weak and frail with no strength or goodness of our own. We need the truths of God's Word applied moment by moment to our hearts. We need time with God in prayer just to conquer the demands of daily life. We need His grace and forgiveness, for without these we are without hope and lost. We can learn to forgive others when we understand that God is willing and ready to forgive us. God desires to remake us, reshape us, into the image of Jesus Christ. When we understand that this is His purpose for us, we can gratefully accept everything that touches our lives. The process may be painful, but the final product will be presented to Him before His throne.

WE LEARN TO SEE OTHERS

Many Christians need us to remind them to look to the Savior, to teach them to trust Him as their guide, to rejoice with them in worship, and to encourage their tired hearts as they serve the Master.

We Learn to See Those Who Haven't Met Our Savior

Wasn't this Jesus' priority in coming to this earth? He came to seek and to save those who are lost (Luke 19:10). His mission should be yours and mine. Remember, dear friend, our souls must daily be restored and refreshed, not for our glory but for His.

❂〉〉〉 ❂〉〉〉 ❂〉〉〉 ❂〉〉 Our Glorious Hope 〈〈❂ 〈〈〈〈❂ 〈〈〈❂ 〈〈〈〈❂

> And if children, then heirs; heirs of God, and joint-heirs with Christ; if so be that we suffer with him, that we may be also glorified together. For I reckon that the sufferings of this present time are not worthy to be compared with the glory which shall be revealed in us. For the earnest expectation of the creature waiteth for the manifestation of the sons of God. (Romans 8:17–19)

One day all the struggles of this life will be over. The discouragement, physical pain, conflicts, and trials will all be set aside when we enter the presence of our Savior. In Romans 8, Paul gives welcome news to our weary hearts. We Christians have a glorious hope in Christ's work on the cross. We may suffer in this life, but our suffering will be turned to glory when we step into His presence. His glory will be revealed in us. "This looks forward to the resurrection of the body (v. 23) and the subsequent complete Christlikeness which is the believer's eternal glory. . . . When Christ returns, God's children will share His glory."[1] God's restoration process concludes with this precious promise: "But we all, with [unveiled] face beholding as in a [mirror] the glory of the Lord, are [transformed] into the same image from glory to glory, even as by the Spirit of the Lord" (2 Corinthians 3:18).[2]

My Heart Restored

I have shared my stories with you. You have perhaps learned the facts—the promises of God's Word that brought me through. You may face similar struggles, but your story will be different.

You must learn from your lessons delivered by God's loving hand. My sharing may have given you direction and encouragement for the trying times. But you must learn from your suffering as I learn from mine. My lessons you can hear, but yours you will see. Oh, how glorious it is to see Him! "I have heard of thee by the hearing of the ear: but now mine eye seeth thee" (Job 42:5).

Let's live this life rejoicing in the hope of the day we stand clothed in His glory! Until that grand day, may we graciously welcome all that He allows to touch our lives. It will be worth it all when we stand in His presence—our heart forever restored.

It will be worth it all when we stand in His presence

Notes

CHAPTER 2—DO I NEED RESTORING?

1. Elizabeth George, *The Lord Is My Shepherd* (Eugene, OR: Harvest House Publishers, 2000), 196.
2. Blue Letter Bible. *The Names of God in the Old Testament*. 1 Apr 2002. 2 Jul 2008. <http://blueletterbible.org/study/misc/name_god.html.
3. Thomas Ward, *Learning to Worship His Name* (Middletown, DE: Partners in Ministry, 2002), i.

CHAPTER 3—HE RESTORES MY SOUL

1. Ward, 6.
2. Ibid.
3. Ibid.

CHAPTER 4—RENEWED THROUGH THE WORD

1. *King James Study Bible* (Nashville: Thomas Nelson, 1981), 1919.

CHAPTER 5—REDIRECTED THROUGH HIS WORD

1. *King James Study Bible*, 1842.
2. Fred and Ruth Coleman, "As We Read Your Holy Word," *A Quiet Heart* (Greenville, SC: Soundforth, 2006).

CHAPTER 6—REFRESHED IN HIS PRESENCE

1. William and Winkie Pratney, *The Daniel Files*. Self-published 1997. http://compsoc.net/~gemini/daniel_files/percept.htm.
2. Judy and Arthur Halliday, *Thin Within* (Nashville: W Publishing Group, 2002), 184.
3. Jerry Bridges, *Transforming Grace* (Colorado Springs: NavPress, 1991), 36.
4. Ronald F. Youngblood, gen. ed., *Nelson's New Illustrated Bible Dictionary* (Nashville: Thomas Nelson, 1997).

5. William Bradbury, "Sweet Hour of Prayer," *Majesty Hymns* (Greenville, SC: Majesty Music, 1996), 437.

CHAPTER 7—RESTING IN HIS GRACE

1. Bridges, 138.
2. Ibid.
3. Charles C. Ryrie, *The Grace of God* (Chicago: Moody Press, 1963), 49.
4. Ibid., 24.
5. Halliday, 99.
6. John Piper, *Pierced by the Word* (Sisters, OR: Multnomah Publishers, 2003), 99–100.
7. Bridges, 21–22.
8. Ibid., 138.
9. Ibid., 84.
10. John Blanchard quoted in Bridges, 145.

CHAPTER 8—RESTORED THROUGH HIS FORGIVENESS

1. *The American Heritage Dictionary*, 4th ed., s.v. "abundantly."
2. *The American Heritage Dictionary*, 4th ed., s.v. "forbearance."
3. Bridges, 203.

CHAPTER 9—REMADE IN HIS LIKENESS

1. Audrey Mieir, "His Name Is Wonderful," *Majesty Hymns* (Greenville, SC: Majesty Music, 1996), 24.
2. Bridges, 112.
3. *King James Study Bible*, 1086.

CHAPTER 10—REACHING OUT TO OTHERS

1. *King James Study Bible*, 1961.

CHAPTER 11—REJOICING IN HOPE

1. John MacArthur, *The MacArthur Study Bible* (Nashville: Word Publishing, 1997), 1708.
2. *King James Study Bible*, 1795–96.

My Heart

RESTORED

STUDY GUIDE

CHAPTER ONE

A Time to Reflect

No matter our age or responsibilities, we all can be "weary in well doing." These times of discouragement should not surprise us. But when we do struggle, how we deal with them will determine their impact on our lives.

MY HEART

1. How would you describe a heart that needs restored?

2. What recent events or circumstances in the world have left you weary, discouraged, or worried? In your community? In your family or personal life?

MY HEART REVEALED

3. In what areas do you need victory and/or encouragement?

4. What do you do when you become overwhelmed with things in your life?

HIS HEART REFLECTED

5. Read Hebrews 12:1–3. What did Jesus endure?

MY HEART RESTORED

6. How would you describe your relationship with the Lord?

7. Can you think of a time in your life that you were closer to the Lord than you are today? If so, when?

8. Describe your "rocking chair place" where you can quietly meet with the Lord.

9. If you don't have a quiet place, where could you make one?

10. In what ways does your heart need restored.

Take each need to the Lord in prayer. Ask Him to begin to restore your heart. Ask Him to show you how to deal honestly with your needs, sins, and attitudes. Thank Him for the joy that awaits your refreshed soul.

CHAPTER TWO — *My Heart Revealed*

The Lord Jesus is the source and power of true restoration for our weary hearts. When we admit we are weak, He can restore our weary heart and give us purpose and strength.

MY HEART REVEALED

1. Elijah gave God eloquent excuses for his actions. What excuses have you given to God?

2. What gets in your way of seeing God and being quiet before Him?

3. In Psalm 3, David describes his enemies. How would you describe the people, circumstances, or attitudes that seem to be your enemies?

4. What did Jesus identify as the solution to Martha's problem?

5. Is sitting at Jesus' feet in Bible study, prayer, and meditation a priority in your life?

HIS HEART REFLECTED

6. In Isaiah 40:28–31, how is God's strength described?

7. How did Jesus' response to Martha reveal His understanding of her need?

MY HEART RESTORED

8. What should you change in your life to put your priorities in Christ-honoring order?

9. How would you complete each statement based on the details of your current situation?

I feel alone like Elijah did because . . .

I am afraid like David was because I am afraid of . . .

My fellowship with God is broken because of the sin of . . .

I need encouragement and help as Moses did because I am
tired of . . .

I am overwhelmed like Martha with the demands of . . .

10. Which Bible character(s) in this chapter did you identify with
    the most?

Review how God worked in the heart of the person you chose.
Share the details of your need with the Lord in prayer. Confess the
sins that you now realize are keeping you defeated. Ask the Lord
for His grace and wisdom to deal with the other issues as He would
want you to.

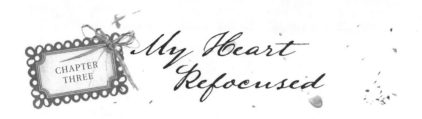

CHAPTER THREE

My Heart Refocused

We must run with patience the pathway of life that the Lord Jesus has given us. But He does not ask us to travel this trail alone. In fact, He knows that we will never endure without His presence.

1. Psalm 69 is another of David's psalms that reveals a struggle in his heart. In Psalm 69:1–5, how did David describe himself and his need?

2. Why did David's heart need restored?

MY HEART REVEALED

3. What did David ask God to do for him, according to Psalm 69:13–18?

4. What areas of your life are taking your focus away from God?

5. What is your normal response to the troubles you face? How should you respond according to 1 Thessalonians 5:18?

HIS HEART REFLECTED

6. What is revealed in Psalm 69:33–36 about God's concern for David and His readiness to help?

7. Hebrews 12:1–3 says we are to focus on whom in times of difficulty?

8. What two phrases from Hebrews 12:1–3 indicate Jesus' role in the encouragement you desire?

MY HEART RESTORED

9. Praise was a major part of David's restorative process. For what was David praising God in Psalm 69:30–32?

10. Using Psalm 69:13–18, 29–34 as a guide, make David's prayer yours by writing it out in your own words.

CHAPTER FOUR

My Heart Renewed

Through diligent study of the Word, God reveals precious truths that will help us walk through this life with encouragement and hope. He renews us through His Word as we read, study, and apply it to our life.

1. In Isaiah 55:10–13, how is God's Word described?

2. What benefit does this analogy describe?

My Heart Revealed

3. What did the Word of God mean to the psalmist according to Psalm 119:25–40?

4. Which of these descriptions best describes your relationship to the Bible?

His Heart Reflected

   5. Read Isaiah 55:10–13 again. What does God want to accomplish through His Word?

My Heart Restored

   6. According to Ephesians 3:20 complete the following statement to fit what you are facing today: Because God desires to work in ways far beyond my comprehension, I need to trust Him completely in regard to . . .

   7. Read Colossians 3:23 and complete the following statement: As a service to the Lord and not to receive praise from others, I need to . . .

   Spend some time in prayer asking the Lord to show you your attitude and approach to His Word. What changes should you make with His help?

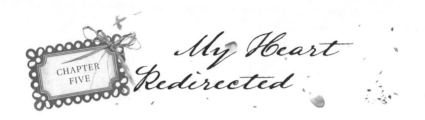

CHAPTER FIVE

My Heart Redirected

The Bible redirects our uncertain steps by helping us see our circumstances from God's point of view. The hope and guidance we find on the pages of Scripture transform times of trial and waiting into seasons of blessing.

1. According to Psalm 119:5, 30, 59, 105, 168, how does God's Word direct man's steps?

MY HEART REVEALED

2. Are you daily in God's Word? Think back over this past week. Which days were harder than others to spend time with God? Why?

3. What areas of your time with God need improvement? Documenting what you learned? Applying what you learned? Consistently studying the Word? Memorizing God's Word?

4. What goals should you set to make the right changes?

His Heart Reflected

5. Read 2 Timothy 3:16–17 and Romans 15:4 and note God's purpose for giving us His written Word.

6. Who is the living Word referred to in John 1:1–5, 14 and Revelation 19:13?

My Heart Restored

7. Read 1 Thessalonians 5:18. How should you finish the following statement to fit what you are facing today? Although what I am facing is difficult, I need to thank God for . . .

8. Read 2 Timothy 1:7. God offers His power to overcome what overwhelms me, His love to love the unlovable, His wisdom to choose what is best. I should not be afraid of . . .

9. What is something that Satan tempts you with? Using a concordance, find some verses that apply to this temptation.

10. What new goals should you set for your Bible study time?

Memorize the verses you found above so that you can apply them the next time Satan tempts you in this area. Pray that God will bring the verses to mind when you need them.

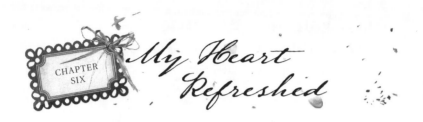

CHAPTER SIX

My Heart Refreshed

When we know God as our Savior and friend, the time we spend in prayer will comfort and encourage us. He is glorified when we come to Him with our needs, our sorrows, our longings, and our praise. When we go to God in prayer, our weary heart is refreshed so that we can continue to serve God and minister to others.

1. What do the following verses teach about God's presence: Deuteronomy 31: 6, 8; Psalm 73:23; Matthew 28:20?

2. In Psalm 28, David tells us what he learned about God's silence. How did David describe God in verses 1 and 7?

3. How might David have responded to God's silence?

4. How did David's outlook change when he realized God heard his prayer (verses 6–9)?

My Heart Revealed

5. List the burdens in your life that you usually pick back up
after praying about them.

His Heart Reflected

6. What are the details of Jesus' prayer time in Mark 1:32–39?
What took place just before and just after His time alone
with God the Father?

7. According to 1 Samuel 15:22 and Jeremiah 9:23–24, what are
God's delights? Do you rejoice in these too?

My Heart Restored

8. Your prayers should include praise to God. What do Psalm
100:4 and 107:8 teach you about praising God?

Take a few moments and review your times of prayer the past
few days. What answers to prayer have you seen in the past few
weeks or months? What blessings or encouragement has the Lord
given you as a result of your time in His presence through prayer?

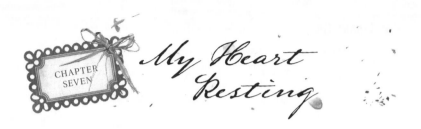

CHAPTER SEVEN

My Heart Resting

God gives rest when we allow Him to minister His grace to us and to make us an instrument of grace to others. Walking in the grace of God will give us peace even in the midst of great trials. God freely offers us His grace and with His grace comes rest.

1. How would you finish this sentence based on the truths in the following verses: 1 Corinthians 15:10; 2 Corinthians 4:15; 12:9; 2 Timothy 2:1? Grace enables us to serve . . .

MY HEART REVEALED

2. What has God's grace done for you?

3. What have you done for someone that illustrates your desire to be gracious to others like God is to you?

4. Colossians 4:6 states that our words should "be always with grace" (gracious) and "seasoned with salt" (wise). Give a situation that your words illustrate this.

His Heart Reflected

5. What do Psalm 84:11 and John 1:17 reveal about the source of grace?

My Heart Restored

6. Using what you learned about God's grace, write out a definition of grace that can be applied to your service to God and to your relationship with others.

7. How should understanding grace change how you serve others?

8. What are you presently facing that you need to step back and watch God work?

Take a moment and pray a heartfelt prayer of surrender to the Lord. Ask Him to work in and through you for His glory. Thank Him for graciously working as He sees best. Be very specific in your surrender and praise, but very open to however He chooses to answer.

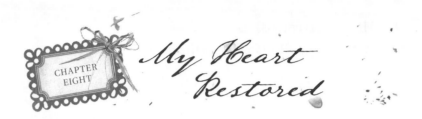

My Heart Restored

Forgiveness comes when we willfully set aside both our pride and the offense. When we confess our sin to Him, God promises not only to forgive but to do so abundantly. He restores our fellowship with Him when our sin is confessed and forgiven and when we forgive others.

1. What truths about forgiveness do Matthew 6:14–15 and 18:21–22 teach?

My Heart Revealed

2. What sins do you excuse because of your circumstances?

3. Read carefully the story of forgiveness in Matthew 18:21–35. List the order of events in Jesus' parable about forgiveness. What lesson was Jesus teaching the disciples?

4. How has the Lord Jesus shown forgiveness and forbearance to you?

5. How would the Lord want you to respond to those you find difficult to forgive or be patient with?

His Heart Reflected

6. How was God's forbearance displayed in Luke 23:33–34?

My Heart Restored

7. Whom have you shown forgiveness or forbearance to in the last week?

8. Whom in your life do you still need to forgive? What should you do to take care of this?

Spend some time in prayer asking the Lord to reveal any unconfessed sin in your life. Ask the Lord to forgive you for all the sins He brings to mind. Ask Him to make you sensitive to the Holy Spirit's conviction and quick to confess and forsake your sin. Thank the Lord for the forbearance and forgiveness He has shown to you.

CHAPTER NINE

My Heart Remade

All the events of life, even the seasons of weariness, are avenues for the grace of God to transform our lives. He remakes us into His likeness through a daily process that involves a continuous conforming of our life to His image. This process will be complete when we go to heaven to be with Him.

1. What do Deuteronomy 8:6 and 5:33 teach us about walking in God's way?

2. The Bible clearly states that man was created in the image of God. According to Mark 12:30, what are the four areas created in us after His image?

MY HEART REVEALED

3. According to Colossians 3:1–2 where should your affections be? What areas in your life are focused on this world instead of God?

4. To be more Christlike, what should you "put off" and "put on" according to Colossians 3:5–17?

HIS HEART REFLECTED

5. What do we learn from Philippians 2:1–8 about the mind of Christ?

MY HEART RESTORED

6. If you submit to God's hand, He will make you into a vessel that brings Him glory. In Jeremiah 18:1–6 what does God compare us to?

7. Jeremiah 18:1–6 also details the role of the wheel in the making of a pot. God uses wheels in various forms and venues in your life. What circumstances has God used to shape you? How did you change to be more like Christ throughout that time?

Thank God for loving you enough to continue to work in your life after you were saved. Spend some time in prayer surrendering to His shaping you into His likeness.

CHAPTER TEN

My Heart Sharing

Our hearts may need restoring because we possess an unloving attitude toward other Christians or a cold indifference to the unsaved. He restores us as we befriend those around us whether they know the Lord as Savior or not. Through the love we share with other Christians, we are encouraged in Who God is and are a testimony to a lost and dying world.

1. What challenge do Proverbs 17:17 and John 15:12 give us in the area of friendship?

MY HEART REVEALED

2. What have you done lately for others? Christian friend? Acquaintance? Unsaved co-worker? Neighbor?

3. How often do you praise God? Do your friends think of you as one who sees God's hand in your circumstances or one who only sees your misery?

4. Who was the last person you shared the gospel with? Discipled? Invited to church?

His Heart Reflected
5. Find in each of these verses an attribute of God that you can rejoice in: Psalm 21:13; Romans 5:8; Philippians 4:7, 19.

6. According to Matthew 9:36–38, how did Jesus respond to the lost souls around Him? To the quarreling disciples?

7. To whom did Jesus have a heart of friendship in John 15:14–15?

My Heart Restored
8. List the wonderful works you can praise God for.

What can you do to build a genuine friendship with those you should be witnessing to? How will this relationship help you to be a more effective witness to them? Begin to pray for opportunities to build friendships with those who don't know the Lord.

My Heart
Rejoicing

The more we practice these restorative steps, the quicker we find peace. When we recognize our need and seek our Savior, we come through the difficult time comprehending more of our sinfulness and more of our Savior's greatness. We may suffer in this life, but our suffering will be turned to glory when we step into His presence. Let's live rejoicing in this hope!

1. According to Psalms 33:21; 104:31; Luke 6:22–23; 10:20, what should make you rejoice?

MY HEART REVEALED

2. Look again at the list of verses from the previous question. Do you rejoice in these areas? What else should make you rejoice?

3. According to Titus 2:13, what should you be looking forward to?

4. If you live with the hope of this future, how will it be reflected in your actions?

His Heart Reflected

5. Romans 8:15–18 reveals the abundant inheritance that you have in Christ. Describe this relationship you have with God.

My Heart Restored

6. The following verses tell of our glorious hope. What does each verse tell about our future: Psalm 16:11; 2 Corinthians 3:18; Colossians 3:4; 1 John 3:2?

7. How will you use the truths you've learned throughout this book to keep your heart rejoicing and restored?

Spend some time in your rocking chair place asking God to show you how you can daily know the joy of a heart restored.